COMMON BACKYARD

Weeds

of the Upper Midwest

T0273446

by Teresa Marrone

Adventure Publications
Cambridge, Minnesota

ACKNOWLEDGMENTS

Cover, book design and illustrations by Jonathan Norberg

Page layout by Teresa Marrone

Edited by Brett Ortler

Photo credits by photographer and page number:
Cover photos: main photo a Clover; inset photo Groundsel; back cover Ground Ivy
All photos by Teresa Marrone unless noted.
All photos are copyright of their respective photographers.

8, *Rhizomes*, John D. Byrd, Mississippi State University, Bugwood.org. **9**, *Yellow Nutsedge root system*, lower left, John Cardina, The Ohio State University, Bugwood.org. **9**, *Strawberry plant stolons*, upper right, ©2014 Jean Pawek. **41**, *Creeping Jenny*, inset, Louis-M. Landry. **47**, *Common Purslane*, inset, Photo courtesy of Debra Cook. **69**, *Field Pennycress*, inset, Keir Morse. **71**, *Garlic Mustard*, inset, Leslie J. Mehrhoff, University of Connecticut, Bugwood. org. **77**, *Fragrant Bedstraw*, right inset, Mary Ellen (Mel) Harte, Bugwood.org. **87**, *Balkan Catchfly*, upper right, Keir Morse. **91**, *Dog Fennel*, right, Photo courtesy of Debra Cook. **91**, *Dog Fennel*, right inset, Keir Morse. **97**, *Poison Hemlock*, left inset, Dr. Mark S. Brunell. **101**, *Venice Mallow*, top, Howard F. Schwartz, Colorado State University, Bugwood.org. **101**, *Venice Mallow*, inset, Lynn Sosnoskie, University of Georgia, Bugwood.org. **107**, *Japanese Knotweed*, left, Karan A. Rawlins, University of Georgia, Bugwood.org. **107**, *Japanese Knotweed*, upper right, Leslie J. Mehrhoff, University of Connecticut, Bugwood.org. **107**, *Japanese Knotweed*, inset, Joseph M. DiTomaso, University of California-Davis, Bugwood.org. **115**, *Wild Parsnip*, upper right, Leslie J. Mehrhoff, University of Connecticut, Bugwood.org. **123**, *Curly Dock*, lower left, Keir Morse. **125**, *St. John's Wort*, left, John Cardina, The Ohio State University, Bugwood.org. **125**, *St. John's Wort*, upper right, Rob Routledge, Sault College, Bugwood.org. **125**, *St. John's Wort*, lower right, Norman E. Rees, USDA Agricultural Research Service-Retired, Bugwood.org. **125**, *St. John's Wort*, inset, Keir Morse. **133**, *Sulfur Cinquefoil*, right, Keir Morse. **149**, *Common Mallow*, upper inset, Keir Morse. **149**, *Common Mallow*, lower inset, Ohio State Weed Lab, The Ohio State University, Bugwood.org. **165**, *Plumeless Thistle*, lower right, Todd Pfeiffer, Klamath County Weed Control, Bugwood.org. **177**, *Climbing False Buckwheat*, right inset, Keir Morse. **181**, *Japanese Hops*, top & inset, Leslie J. Mehrhoff, University of Connecticut, Bugwood.org. **185**, *Bur Cucumber*, inset, Pamela B. Trewatha.**189**, *Common Morning Glory*, upper right, Howard F. Schwartz, Colorado State University, Bugwood.org. **189**, *Ivy-Leaved Morning Glory*, lower right, Rebekah D. Wallace, University of Georgia, Bugwood.org

10 9 8 7

Photo credits continued on page 216

Common Backyard Weeds of the Upper Midwest
Copyright © 2017 by Teresa Marrone
Published by Adventure Publications
An imprint of AdventureKEEN
310 Garfield Street South
Cambridge, Minnesota 55008
(800) 678-7006
www.adventurepublications.net
All rights reserved
Printed in China
ISBN 978-1-59193-732-6 (pbk.); 978-1-59193-706-7 (ebook)

TABLE OF CONTENTS

INTRODUCTION

About This Book 4

How to Use This Book 5

What is a Weed? 6

Native vs. Non-native Plants 6

Plant Biology for Beginners 8

Identifying Plants Visually 10

Getting Rid of Weeds 18

CREEPING AND LOW-GROWING WEEDS 22

UPRIGHT BROADLEAF WEEDS 56

VINING WEEDS 174

GRASSLIKE WEEDS 190

RECOMMENDED REFERENCES 206

INDEX 207

A NOTE ABOUT CONSUMING WILD PLANTS 215

ABOUT THE AUTHOR 216

ABOUT THIS BOOK

Common Backyard Weeds of the Upper Midwest is written primarily for homeowners, not botanists, farmers or turf managers. That's not to say that botanists, farmers and turf managers won't find it interesting and useful. What it means is that this book approaches weeds from the layperson's perspective rather than from the perspective of someone who deals with plants professionally.

While you'll find a few simple technical terms scattered throughout, plant descriptions are written in plain, simple language that is easy to understand, even if you haven't studied botany. Many books approach plants using the classic taxonomic organization. With this system, if you want to identify a weed in your yard, you must first identify the family to which it belongs, then determine the genus and finally—if you're lucky—the exact species. So if you have a weedy plant with, say, four white petals, you may have to flip through several chapters to find something that resembles your specimen.

This book is organized by the visual characteristics of the plants, starting first with its growth pattern (creeping and low-growing, upright, vining, grassy) and then considering the color of the flower. Although it is a bit non-scientific (and will no doubt drive botanists crazy), that's the most intuitive way for the non-scientist to identify a plant. Looking at the photos in this book and comparing them to your plant, you'll find a dozen or more common weeds whose flowers have four white petals, along with text describing some look-alikes. By studying the photos and accompanying text, you should be able to identify your plant (if it is a common weed, that is)—or at least learn enough about it to delve deeper with a more comprehensive reference.

Clear photos show the parts or stages of the plant that will help get you on track to identify it. The text gives enough detail to help you learn what characteristics you need to look at for identification, without being bogged down by a lot of technical terms you may have to scramble to decipher.

What is Not Included

Because this book is written for homeowners, it does not include crop pests and other **agricultural weeds** that are unlikely to appear in the yard or garden. Note that a number of agricultural weeds do, indeed, grow in home settings, and many of those are included in this book.

It also does not include **aquatic weeds**. Some shoreline weeds that appear in damp areas along lakes or rivers may be found in backyards that abut natural areas (or that have, say, a small pond), so a few of these are included; in particular, Purple Loosestrife is featured because it is a highly invasive shoreline plant that should be eradicated wherever it is found—and that might be your backyard, if your property is close to water.

Shrubs and trees are often weedy, but are not included in this book, which concentrates on non-woody plants. Similarly, **mushrooms** and other non-vascular plants such as **moss and lichens** are not discussed; those are subjects for a different book. (For shrubs and trees, I might suggest my series of *Wild Berries and Fruits Field Guide* books, which are available for all states in this region; each book covers three states in our area. For mushrooms, check out *Mushrooms of the Upper Midwest*, a photographic ID guide I coauthored with fellow mushroom enthusiast Kathy Yerich. See information on pg. 216.)

HOW TO USE THIS BOOK

1. Determine what type of plant your weed is: creeping or low-growing, upright broadleaf, vine, or grass. Go to the start of that category.
2. Categories except grasses are organized by the **color of the flower**, in this order: green, white, yellow, orange, pink/red and purple. Find the start of the appropriate color; for example, broadleaf plants with yellow flowers start on pg. 108.
3. Plants with flowers of a similar color are ordered approximately by the **season in which the plant flowers**, starting with spring. Study the photos and compare them to your plant; if flowers aren't present, you may have to go through the entire category.
4. Also read the COMPARE information for other plants that have similar attributes to the one in the photos.
5. Some plants are listed as having edible parts. Please read "A note about consuming wild plants" on pg. 215 before eating any weeds.

WHAT IS A WEED?

Most people have heard the common saying that "a weed is a plant that is growing where it is not wanted." In many cases, that simple truth says it all. Many of the plants in the book are considered wildflowers, and we enjoy seeing plants such as buttercups, violets or daisies growing wild in the woods. When they settle into our gardens and carefully landscaped areas, however, we often consider them weedy and unwanted.

Some native plants, such as Horseweed (pg. 98) and Peppergrass (pg. 72), are gangly or unattractive, and are acceptable in the woods but not the backyard. Other native plants, like Poison Ivy (pgs. 60 and 174), cause misery for humans and are unwelcome even in many wild settings, not to mention in the garden.

NATIVE VS. NON-NATIVE PLANTS

All plants in this book are identified as either native or non-native. This is an important distinction, because non-native plants are more likely to become a problem weed than native plants are—although plenty of native plants can turn into garden pests as well. These terms mean exactly what they sound like. Native plants are those that evolved in the U.S. on their own; they were here long before the first Europeans set foot on U.S. soil, and many were used by Native peoples as food, for medicine, for cordage and for other uses. Non-native plants are sometimes called **introduced**, because they were brought to this country, typically from Asia or Europe, deliberately or accidentally.

Some plants are brought deliberately from other countries because they were good food crops in their native countries; these are agricultural plants, and include wheat and potatoes as well as a number of now-common grains, fruits and vegetables. Other plants are imported as horticultural specimens, for their beauty; these are commonly sold in garden centers. Unfortunately, both agricultural and horticultural plants that are non-native may escape their intended planting areas. When they do, there may be no natural enemies, such as insects or native wildlife, to keep them in check, and they can spread rampantly, becoming invasive. More on that in a minute.

Accidental introduction from other countries happens when seeds from a plant creep into shipping containers, or become mixed with desirable grains. Seeds may also hitch a ride in packing materials, such as straw, that are used to protect fragile goods during shipment from, say, India or China to the U.S. Some plants or seeds are brought over illicitly; for example, marijuana is often smuggled into the U.S. from Mexico and South America, and it has become an agricultural pest in several states in our region.

Weeds can also be transported from the U.S. to other countries, often becoming a problem in their new locations. Horseweed, for example, has been a nuisance in parts of Europe for a very long time. Many believe that Horseweed seeds were nestled in animal pelts that were shipped to Europe by the Voyageurs, a group of mostly French-Canadians who trapped fur-bearing animals in Canada and the northern states around the Great Lakes from the late seventeenth to the early nineteenth centuries.

About Invasive and Noxious Plants

A plant is considered **invasive** when it spreads aggressively and displaces desirable native flora. Most invasive plants are non-native, including Purple Loosestrife (pg. 170), Crown Vetch (pg. 154) and Spotted Knapweed (pg. 168). A **noxious** weed is one that is considered harmful to human health, or which has a tendency to overrun natural areas or agricultural crops. These can be native or non-native, and include such pests as Poison Ivy and Ragweed (pgs. 60 and 58), both of which are native plants, and non-natives such as Queen Anne's Lace (pg. 96) and Bull Thistle (pg. 164).

Invasive and noxious plants can be tough to eradicate from your garden and may be even more difficult to remove from natural areas and agricultural fields. You can help prevent the spread of weeds by staying on established trails when you're walking in parks or forests, and preventing pets from running off the path. Clean your shoes both before and after walking in a natural area, to avoid spreading seeds; many parks have special shoe-cleaning stations at trailheads.

This book includes approximate ranges in our region where the featured plants can be found. Information comes from the U.S.D.A. website at plants.usda.gov and also from the Biota of North America Program at bonap.org. Note that plant ranges change over time. You can find updated distribution at eddmaps.org/distribution/. Type the plant name in the search box and click on the name when it appears in the results box. Next, click on "county," then "record density."

PLANT BIOLOGY FOR BEGINNERS

This book is designed to be easy for the layperson to use, and avoids highly technical descriptions. However, a basic understanding of plant biology is helpful, as some terms that are used in this book might be unfamiliar. First, let's take a look at how plants grow and reproduce.

All flowering plants produce seeds, which can germinate (sprout) to create new plants. Not all plant reproduction happens through seeds, however, and a lot of it has to do with the life cycle of the plant. There are three main life cycles for plants: annual, biennial and perennial.

Annual plants are non-woody plants that reproduce only by seed, and live for just one year. They flower and produce seeds, then the entire plant dies at the end of the growing season. New plants appear the following season when the seeds germinate.

Biennial plants are non-woody plants with a two-year life cycle. In their first year they grow as a ground-hugging, or **basal**, cluster of leaves; the leaves usually die at the end of the growing season but the roots survive until the next season. In the second year, the roots produce an above-ground stem with seed-producing flowers. The second-year plant dies at the end of the growing season, and new plants must be produced by the seeds left behind.

Perennial plants are those that live three or more years. Trees, shrubs and woody vines are perennials, but here we're discussing herbaceous perennials, which have non-woody stems. The top growth (leaves, stems and flowers) usually dies back at the end of the growing season, but the underground root system survives for years, sending up new shoots each year.

Rhizomes between grass clumps

Root systems of perennials take different forms. Many perennials spread by underground stems called **rhizomes** that travel sideways from the main root. Rhizomes have nodes that develop new roots; soon the roots send up a shoot that grows into a new plant. Once the new plant is established, it, too, will send out rhizomes, helping to create an ever-larger patch or colony of the weed. Most rhizomes you'll encounter will look like pale roots that are somewhat thickened.

Stolons (also called runners) are another sideways-traveling stem, but these are aboveground and rather wiry. A stolon can develop roots where it touches the ground; the roots produce shoots that become new plants. As with rhizomes, the new plants can also send out their own stolons,

Stolons on strawberry plant

creating a dense patch of the plant. The strawberry is a familiar plant that spreads by stolons; the thin, hairy brown stems in the photo above are stolons.

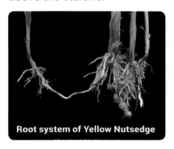

Root system of Yellow Nutsedge

Some plants also have **tubers**, a thickened portion of an underground rhizome or root. The potato is a well-known tuber, although most tubers are not so large. Tubers store starch to feed the plants and also produce nodes or shoots—like the eyes on a potato—that can produce new plants. The photo at left shows the root system of Yellow Nutsedge (pg. 198); it consists of roots, basal bulbs, rhizomes and tubers, which are the small ball-like structures at the bottom of the photo.

Corms, bulbs and tuberous roots are additional types of underground reproductive structures found on some plants, but these are not discussed in this book.

However they reproduce, perennials can be difficult to remove from your garden or other location where you don't want them, because all parts of the root system must be eliminated. Even small, broken-off pieces of rhizomes, stolons or tubers can resprout to produce new plants, so removal methods that break up the roots only create more problems. Most annuals, on the other hand, have shallow roots and are easy to pull, although some develop long taproots that present more of a challenge.

IDENTIFYING PLANTS VISUALLY

Most people are familiar with common garden weeds such as violets and dandelions. But what do you do if something shows up in your garden that you didn't plant and can't identify? Or, perhaps your lawn is being overrun with a weed you're not familiar with. In either case, you need to learn the identity of the plant, so you can decide if you should let it grow or remove it. In this section, we'll take a quick look at the parts of a plant you should study in order to identify it. Rather than go into lengthy descriptions that use a lot of scientific jargon, this book will use photographs, accompanied by short text, to illustrate the various plant parts. We'll go from the ground up.

Leaves

Leaf shape is the first thing to look at, followed by arrangement, then attachment to the stem. Leaf texture and color are identifying factors in some cases, but these concepts are pretty easy to grasp from the descriptions in individual plant accounts and are not shown here.

The most common leaf shapes are shown below and on the facing page. These shapes apply to simple, non-compound leaves, as well as to the leaflets of compound leaves (see pg. 12 for compound leaf configurations). The name used first is somewhat more intuitive, followed in some cases by the more technical name you may see in other references. A short description follows.

LEAF SHAPES

Egg-shaped/ovate
Longer than it is wide, broadest toward the base, pointed tip

Teardrop-shaped/ obovate
Longer than it is wide, broadest toward the tip, tapered base

Elliptic/elliptical
Longer than it is wide, broadest at the middle, curved sides, evenly tapered on both ends

Oblong
Two to three times as long as it is wide, nearly parallel sides, tapered at both ends

Lance-like/lanceolate
Three to four times longer than it is wide, typically broadest below the middle, pointed tip

Linear
Much longer than it is wide, equal width overall, tips may be rounded or pointed

Heart-shaped/cordate
Much wider towards the stalk, base sharply indented to form two rounded lobes, pointed tip

Round/orbicular
Roughly circular in outline, approximately as long as it is wide

Kidney-shaped/ reniform
Roughly semi-circular with indented base, wider than they are long

Arrowhead-shaped/ hastate
Three distinct points, notched at the base, resemble an arrowhead

Deeply lobed
Deep indentations along leaf edges; lobes and leaves may be any overall shape

Shallowly lobed
Shallow indentations along leaf edges; lobes and leaves may be any overall shape

Compound Leaves

A **simple** leaf is undivided and attached to the stem of the plant, either directly or with a stalk that is called a petiole. There will be a bud at the point where the leaf (or its stalk) joins the plant's stem.

Compound leaves have three or more leaflets attached to a leaf stalk. Just as with a simple leaf, there will be a bud at the point where the leaf stalk joins the plant's stem; there are no buds at the leaflet bases. The leaflets may be attached to the leaf stalk directly, or with additional stalks called petiolules.

Leaflets on compound leaves have the same shapes as simple leaves. Some compound leaves are twice compound, or bipinnate; this means that the leaflet is further divided into smaller leaflets.

COMPOUND LEAVES

Trifoliate
Three leaflets are attached to the tip of the leaf stalk

Palmate
Four or more leaflets are attached to the tip of the leaf stalk

Pinnate
Multiple leaflets are attached to an extension of the leaf stalk (called a rachis)

Twice compound/bipinnate
Leaflets on a pinnately compound leaf are further compound

How Leaves are Arranged On the Stems

This describes how the leaves or leaf stalks relate to one another on the main stem. The descriptions apply to both simple and compound leaves, and also to the leaflets found on compound leaves.

LEAF ARRANGEMENT

Opposite
Attached in pairs, directly across from each other

Alternate
Attached singly, spaced out along the main stem

Whorled
Three or more leaves attached to the same point in spoke-like fashion

Attachment To the Stem

This describes how individual leaves are attached to the main stem; the descriptions also apply to the way leaflets are attached to the leaf stalks of a compound leaf.

LEAF ATTACHMENT

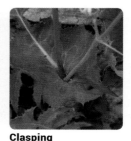

With a stalk (petiole)
Leaves have a distinct stalk that attaches to the main stem; stalk may be long or short

Directly/sessile
Base of the leaf attaches directly to the stem, with no leaf stalk

Clasping
Base of the leaf attaches directly to the stem and wraps around it in a clasping fashion

Stems

Stems can be round, square or angled. They may be smooth, hairy, ribbed, rough, prickly or downy. The descriptions in the individual plant accounts should be sufficient to distinguish the plant, so photos are not included here.

Flowers

Although this is not a book about flowers, the plant accounts in this book include information about the structure, color and abundance of the flowers on each plant. This is because flowers are often the key to identifying a plant.

Like most living things, flowers have male and female parts. Depending on species, they may exist together in a single flower, or may grow on different types of flowers on the same plant (or sometimes on a separate plant).

The female part of a flower is collectively called the **pistil**. It consists of an ovary, topped with a long style that is capped with the stigma. The ovary contains eggs, held in structures called carpels. These are not visible unless the plant is dissected, so they are not shown in the photos here.

The male part of the flower is collectively called the **stamen**. It consists of a pollen-bearing element called the anther, which is supported by the filament, a thin structure that raises the anther above the throat of the flower.

Fertilization occurs when pollen is introduced into the ripe eggs. Pollination is performed by bees and other insects, animals or the wind. The pollen is deposited onto the sticky stigma, where it germinates, sending the male nuclei down the style to fertilize the eggs. The ovary swells as the eggs mature and produces the fruits, which may be seeds, berries, capsules, cones, seedpods or other structures we might not recognize as a fruit.

Most flowers have distinct petals, which are typically colored and attractive; they have naturally evolved to catch the eye of pollinators. Composite flowers such as daisies have two types of petal-like structures that are actually individual florets. These are called disk flowers and ray flowers; see pg. 16 for more details.

Sepals are leaflike structures below the base of the flower; collectively, they are called a **calyx**. The sepals enclose the flower bud before it opens up, and also support the bases of the petals once the flower blooms. Sepals often fold around the seeds that develop from the flowers.

Bracts are modified leaves that are often found at the base of the flowers; they add strength and help protect the flowers. Some bracts are highly colorful; the red "petals" of the poinsettia are actually bracts.

Although the flowers below have different shapes, the various parts are still fairly easy to distinguish when they're visible.

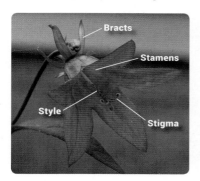

SEVERAL TYPES OF FRUITS (tufted seeds, berries, seedpods, seedhead)

Some plants, such as Clovers (pg. 32), have flowerheads composed of numerous individual tiny flowers, each with male and female parts. However, Clover flowers are so tiny that the overall impression is of a single, round flower. When the individual flowers are viewed under magnification, they can be quite stunning. At the top right, you can see a patch of familiar White Clover flowers; below that is a magnified view of the Alsike Clover flowerhead, which has the same structure as that of White Clover. These flowers are referred to as pea-like because they have the same structure as flowers on garden pea vines.

Pea-like flowers, like those of Birdsfoot Trefoil (photo at left), have 5 petals: a banner, 2 wing petals and 2 keel petals. The banner (also called the standard) is the upper petal, which is erect and is the largest petal. Below that, the 2 cupped wing petals meet in the center of the flower to enclose the 2 keel petals, which are visible if the wing petals are open. The keel petals are joined into a keel-like shape to enclose the pistil and stamens.

Daisies, including the Oxeye Daisy (pg. 90), are called composite flowers because their flowering head consists of two different types of small, specialized flowers called **florets**. The outer florets are called ray flowers; these are the white "petals" that grow in a ring around the central disk, which is composed of tiny, tubular yellow disk florets that produce seeds.

Dandelions (pg. 36) may seem to have a similar structure, but they are composed entirely of flat ray florets, which produce the seeds. If you look closely at a dandelion, you may see the curled stigmas on top of the skinny styles.

How Flowers are Arranged On the Stem

Some weeds, including Oxeye Daisy (opposite page) produce a single flower at the top of a stem. Most, however, have flowers that grow in clusters. Here are the most common configurations.

FLOWER ARRANGEMENT

Raceme
Elongated floral stem with single flowers attached to stemlets of equal length, distributed at equal intervals; flowers mature from the bottom of the stem up

Spike
Similar to a raceme, but the flowers are sessile, meaning they are attached directly to the floral stem with no stemlet

Umbel
Clusters of flowers on stemlets of equal length that originate from the same point on the stem (like umbrella spokes); the tops may be flat or rounded

Corymb
Clusters of flowers on stemlets of varying length that originate from different points on the stem; tops usually flat

Branching clusters or branched stalks
These are not scientific terms; they are used in this book as catchalls to avoid complicated descriptions. Panicles and cymes are scientific terms for two examples.

GETTING RID OF WEEDS

Although dousing everything with potent weed killers may seem like an easy solution, there are other methods to use—and reasons to do so. This section will discuss various options, starting with the least aggressive. Check the species accounts in this book for guidelines on which method to try with the weeds you're hoping to eliminate.

Pulling by Hand

This is the most basic method of removing weeds. It can be very effective on certain weeds, less so on others. Here are a few guidelines.

- **Know your target.** Pulling is often the method of choice for shallow-rooted annuals, first-year basal leaf clusters of biennials, and young shoots of some perennials. With other plants, you risk breaking off the stem, leaving roots and rhizomes behind to produce new plants.
- **Pull when the soil is loose.** The best time to pull weeds is usually the day after a rainfall; you can also sprinkle the area the day before you want to do some weeding. If you try to pull plants out of hard, dry soil, you'll probably leave roots behind.
- **Pull properly.** Grasp the plant at the base—not from the top—and pull straight up.
- **Use a tool as an assistant if necessary.** A narrow trowel, a pronged dandelion digging tool or an old table fork may help loosen a small, stubborn root ball. For larger plants, try a flat-bladed garden fork.
- **Follow the roots.** When pulling weeds such as Ground Ivy (pg. 52) that spread by aboveground runners, follow the runner to the next root node and pull that too, then keep going. You may also be able to follow the underground rhizomes of grasses and other weeds, but the soil has to be really loose. In either case, grasp the root nodes right at the soil and gently tease them out rather than pulling on the stems.
- **Pull before the flowers go to seed.** You don't want to scatter seeds around while you're pulling; nor do you want the wind to do the scattering for you. Get those weeds out before they produce seeds.
- **Fill in the hole.** When you pull a weed, you are creating a spot that is ripe for takeover by any weed seeds that happen to land there. Fill in even small holes, and sprinkle grass seed or mulch over the bare dirt.
- **Bag seedy weeds.** If you've pulled weeds that have gone to seed, bag and dispose of them rather than composting; unless a compost pile is extremely hot, most seeds will survive. Municipal composting

operations may be hot enough to handle weed seeds; check with your municipality if this type of composting is offered.

- **Check the area again in a week or two.** New shoots may have sprouted, and they are easy to pull when young. You'll have to remain vigilant, sometimes for several years, as seeds from some plants can germinate even after many years in the soil.

Mowing

If the weeds you're after are in the lawn or an area where mowing is practical, it is a good option for some species. Read on for some tips.

- **Mow at the right time.** Mow when flowers are present, but before seeds have developed. This is particularly important with perennials, because a plant in bloom has a lot of energy invested in those flowers, and you will starve the roots by mowing at that time.
- **Don't mow too low.** Low mowing weakens quality turf grasses, giving weedy grasses a competitive edge. Longer grass also keeps soil cooler and allows less sunlight to penetrate to low-growing weeds. A mowing height of 2½ to 3 inches usually works well, but check with your county extension agent for recommendations for your area.
- **Keep an eye on the area.** If you've mowed where there were tall weeds, check the area again in a day or two. Some weeds may have been knocked over by the mower but not cut off, and you can pull them once they stand upright.
- **It's not a one-time thing.** Mowing often needs to be repeated several times throughout the season as plants regrow from roots left behind.

Digging

Now we are talking about getting into more serious work—and potentially, creating new problems, because whenever you dig, you unearth dormant weed seeds, bringing them up from the depths into areas where they get enough light and moisture to sprout. But if you've got a patch of perennial weeds, digging is the best non-chemical option.

- **Choose the right tool.** A flat-bottomed spade isn't much use for digging up tough roots. A sharp-tipped shovel is a better choice because it allows you to get down into the soil and under the roots. A small hand trowel with a pointed tip works well for small root clusters.
- **Get the whole root system.** Rhizomes can regrow from pieces as small as an inch. If you're going to dig them up, get as much of the rhizome as you can, or you'll have to do it again the following season.

- **Cut off taproots.** Thistles and other biennials have deep taproots that will resprout in the same season if only the aboveground growth is pulled or mowed. Cut off the taproot by driving the tip of a sharp shovel into the ground at an angle, right next to the plant's stem. You want to cut off the taproot as far below the soil as possible; try to get 6 inches down. Now pull out the stem and fill the hole with dirt.

Flaming

If you haven't heard of this technique, you're not alone. But it can be surprisingly effective in removing clumps of weeds without chemicals. Weed burners are handheld wands that use propane to produce a very hot flame—up to 2,000°F—that literally cooks the weed's leaves and stems in a second or less. They work great on annuals; perennials may require additional sessions. There are many precautions involved in using a spot flame to burn weeds; this method isn't suitable for all locations, and can't be used safely in dry conditions. But if you're desperate to remove weeds without chemicals or digging, you may want to look into one of these; be sure to read and follow all instructions.

Herbicides

Home centers are replete with a variety of weed-killing chemicals. Here are some things to consider when choosing this method.

- **Know when to use various types.** Preemergent herbicides must be applied just before the target weed germinates; they don't work once the plants are up. Similarly, glyphosate and some other non-selective post-emergent herbicides work only when they are in direct contact with the weed's leaves or stems; they don't prevent germination.
- **Protect other plants.** Non-selective herbicides like glyphosate will kill any plants they contact (except those that have been genetically engineered to resist it, and some weeds that have built up natural resistance over time). Cover other plants with plastic before spraying.
- **Take a targeted approach.** If you've got Bindweed or other vines to deal with, get a plastic water tube from a florist (these are small tubes that can be filled with water; they have a rubber cap with a small hole for a flower stem). Fill it with an appropriate liquid herbicide, then slip the tip of the vine into the hole so the vine will drink in the herbicide.
- **Consider organics.** Cornmeal gluten is a totally natural corn byproduct that can be scattered over the lawn in spring. It acts as a

preemergent to stop weed seeds from germinating and inhibits root growth. It can take several years of application to see results.

- **Always follow label directions.** This is not a case of "if a little is good, more is better." Apply the product exactly as specified on the label.
- **Consider the whole ecosystem.** Before using toxic chemicals, try to learn what impact it might have on soil microorganisms, bees, birds, fish and humans. Note that DDT was considered a safe pesticide until studies in the 1950s and 1960s confirmed the link between DDT and declining bird populations. Herbicides in common use today may be responsible for similar damage, and some are also being studied for possible links to human woes including reproductive damage and cancer. Chemicals that are widely used today may well be the next DDT. Stay informed, and consider less toxic options.

Stop Weeds Before They Grow

It is a lot easier to prevent weeds from growing than to pull them. Here are a few simple things you can try.

- **Organic mulch**, such as wood chips, will prevent new weeds from growing in an area you've cleaned up—but only if you use at least 2 inches of it. Don't pile mulch directly against the bases of trees and shrubs. Consider putting breathable landscape fabric down before adding the mulch, for another level of protection and prevention.
- **Overseeding** (sprinkling grass seed on a patchy or weedy lawn) is an important long-term strategy to prevent weeds from taking over. Do this in fall, so the new grass can germinate in the spring. This seems like a small thing, but over time, it can help you win the war against common lawn weeds such as Ground Ivy and Ragweed.
- **Soil amendments** such as composted manure and fertilizer also encourage vigorous growth of desirable garden plants and lawn grasses, allowing them to outcompete weeds that may try to move in. Look for amendments at any garden store. As a natural option, you could try watering or spraying garden plants and grasses with compost tea; search online for directions explaining how to make and use it.

As a final note, always remember that vigorous, healthy growth of desirable plants will prevent many weeds from becoming established. Weeds are hardwired to fill in the gaps and take advantage of a poorly kept lawn or garden. Don't let it be *your* lawn or garden!

Plantain

(Plantago spp.)*

OVERVIEW: Two similar-looking varieties of this perennial are familiar weedy pests throughout our area. Both grow as a **low cluster of basal leaves with long, thin, nubby-looking spikes arising from the center**.

WHERE YOU'LL FIND IT: Very common in disturbed areas and vacant lots; also found in lawns and landscape plantings. It often grows through pavement cracks (see small photo at right) and likes moderate sun.

LEAVES: Egg-shaped, with a **wide, flat stalk** that can be nearly as long as the blade. Mature leaves are smooth, fairly thick and a bit leathery. **Distinct veins** radiate from the point where the stalk joins the leaf, and the leaves often appear puckered. Edges are typically wavy; a few large, irregular teeth may be present. • Common Plantain (*P. major*; non-native) is found in the northern two-thirds of our region. The basal cluster may be up to a foot across; leaves are 2 to 5 inches long, not including the stalk. • Black-Seeded Plantain (*P. rugelii*), a native variety found throughout our area except the Dakotas, is slightly larger; its basal cluster can reach **14 inches across**, and leaves may be nearly **7 inches long**. The base of the leaf stalk is often **purplish**.

FLOWERS/FRUIT: The floral spikes are **slender and cylindrical**. They can get quite lengthy if the plant isn't mowed over, but are generally 4 to 10 inches long and may be erect or drooping. Inconspicuous green flowers with purple-tipped stamens grow on the upper half of the spike. The flowers are replaced by tiny oval seeds that are **brown** on Common Plantain and **black** on Black-Seeded Plantain.

SEASON: Plantain flowers from early summer through early fall.

OTHER NAMES: Common Plantain is also called Broad-Leaved Plantain.

COMPARE: Non-native English Plantain (*P. lanceolata*) has narrow, **lance-like leaves**; the flowers grow only at the tip of the flowering spike. Common throughout our area except the Dakotas, Minnesota and northern Wisconsin, where scattered populations exist.

GETTING RID OF IT!

Plantain reproduces by both roots and seeds. The roots are short and tough, so hand-pulling can be effective when the soil is moist; pull well before the seeds develop. Because the leaves hug the ground and seeds develop even on short floral spikes, mowing is not an effective control.

WHAT'S IT GOOD FOR?

The leaves are edible and nutritious; they are slightly bitter, and the bitterness increases with maturity. The veins can be tough and are often removed, especially on mature leaves. Young leaves can be eaten raw, while mature leaves are best cooked. The leaves can also be chewed and applied as a poultice to soothe insect bites, burns and small wounds.

Aunt Lucy

(Ellisia nyctelea)

OVERVIEW: This native annual usually grows in sprawling fashion. Its stems may be a bit more than a foot long but are usually quite a bit shorter. Its lacy, many-divided leaves are very distinctive.

WHERE YOU'LL FIND IT: Gardens, disturbed areas, roadsides, compost heaps, next to buildings and retaining walls, along alleys and in woodlands. It prefers areas with partial shade and adequate moisture. Aunt Lucy is found primarily in the center of the U.S., becoming uncommon east of Illinois; in our region it's also absent from northern Minnesota, northern Wisconsin, and all of Michigan.

LEAVES: The leaves are oblong and **deeply lobed**, with up to **13 leaflet-like lobes** per leaf; each lobe has 3 to 5 additional rounded lobes, giving the plant a somewhat **lacy** appearance. Leaves are up to 3½ inches long and covered in **short, bristly hairs**. They grow oppositely on short, thick stemlets at the base of the plant, but alternately at the top.

FLOWERS/FRUIT: Bell-shaped flowers with 5 petals grow on short, hairy stemlets originating at leaf axils on the upper parts of the stems; they typically grow singly and only a few are in bloom at one time. Flowers are about ¼ inch across and ½ inch long; insides are **white with purple spots**. A **hairy, star-shaped cup** surrounds the base of each flower. A hairy pea-size capsule replaces each flower; it is green, becoming brown.

SEASON: Plants appear in very early spring. Flowers are present in late spring through early summer; plants wither away by midsummer.

OTHER NAMES: Waterweed, Waterpod.

COMPARE: At a very quick glance, Aunt Lucy's leaves somewhat resemble those of Rusty Woodsia (*Woodsia ilvensis*), which is found in our region primarily in rocky areas of western Wisconsin and northeastern Minnesota. Rusty Woodsia is a **hairy-leaved fern** that has **no flowers**.

GETTING RID OF IT!

Aunt Lucy grows from a stout taproot that is fairly easy to pull. If you don't want it reappearing the following year, pull the plants before the seed capsules develop.

WHAT'S IT GOOD FOR?

It's a fairly inoffensive plant in most locations, and the flowers are a decent subject for macro photography. Like most flowering plants, it is visited by some bee species.

Mouse-Ear Chickweed (*Cerastium fontanum*)

OVERVIEW: Stems of this non-native perennial may be up to 18 inches long, although they are usually much shorter. They typically sprawl along the ground and may root at the nodes, creating tangled mats. Stems are round and reddish to greenish; they are covered in **fine hairs**.

WHERE YOU'LL FIND IT: It is found in lawns, along roadsides and sidewalks, on prairies, and in woodlands. Very common throughout our region except in the Dakotas, southwestern Minnesota and western Iowa.

LEAVES: The oblong leaves are up to 1 inch long with a deep central vein; **both surfaces are covered with fine hairs**, and the edges are untoothed but hairy. They grow oppositely in pairs and are sessile.

FLOWERS/FRUIT: White flowers about ¼ inch across grow singly or in small clusters; they have 5 petals with **deeply notched tips**. The petals are **longer than the 5 green sepals**, which are visible below the petals. A tubular seed capsule with 10 teeth at the tip replaces each flower.

SEASON: Flowers appear from late spring through early fall.

OTHER NAMES: *C. vulgatum*.

COMPARE: Several other non-native chickweeds are found in our area.
• Common Chickweed (*Stellaria media*) is an annual that is very similar to Mouse-Ear Chickweed in overall appearance and size, but its **egg-shaped** leaves have a **hairless** upper surface. The flowers **appear to have 10 petals** because the lobes are so deeply cleft, and the flower petals are **noticeably shorter than the sepals**. Common Chickweed is slightly less common than Mouse-Ear Chickweed in the northern part of our region. • Giant Chickweed (*Myosoton aquaticum*; also called Water Chickweed) is up to **2 feet** tall. Its flowers are **½ inch** across; like Common Chickweed, the petals are very deeply lobed, but they are **slightly longer than the sepals**. Leaves are up to 2½ inches long and **moderately hairy**. Giant Chickweed is perennial and prefers moist areas; in our region it is found primarily in Minnesota and Wisconsin.

Mouse-Ear
Chickweed

Common Chickweed

GETTING RID OF IT!

Chickweed roots are shallow, and pulling can be effective but must be repeated until all traces of the plants are gone. Perennial chickweeds are more difficult to eliminate than the annual Common Chickweed. If using herbicides, apply in spring before the seeds develop.

WHAT'S IT GOOD FOR?

Young leaves of Common Chickweed are edible raw or cooked; the other two species discussed here are also edible but less favored because of their hairy texture. Some songbirds eat the seeds of various chickweeds; certain bees, butterflies and wasps visit the flowers. Leaves are eaten by deer, rabbits and some birds.

Low-Growing Spurges

(Euphorbia spp.)

OVERVIEW: Two native low-growing Spurges are common in our area. These annuals are sprawling plants with **thin stems** and **tiny leaves**.

WHERE YOU'LL FIND IT: Sunny, dry areas such as abandoned lots and ill-kept boulevards. Frequently grows from cracks in pavement. Both will grow in mulched areas that are not watered frequently.

LEAVES: The Spurges listed here have **opposite** oblong leaves up to ⅝ inch long. All parts of the plant produce **milky sap** when broken. • Spotted Spurge (*E. maculata*) has **hairy** stems that are often reddish. Leaves grow on short stemlets, and are **asymmetrical at the base**. Leaf tips and edges have **small, blunt teeth**. Typically, there is a **red mark** in the middle of each leaf. Found throughout our region except the Dakotas and northwestern Minnesota. • Ridge-Seed Spurge (*E. glyptosperma*) is very similar to Spotted Spurge, but its leaves **lack the red mark** and its stems are **hairless**. Found in the northern two-thirds of our region.

FLOWERS/FRUIT: Tiny flowers about ⅛ inch across, with 4 white to pink petal-like projections surrounding a central cup, grow singly or in small clusters at leaf axils. Flowers are replaced by 3-lobed capsules.

SEASON: Plants with flowers are present from summer through fall.

OTHER NAMES: These plants are sometimes referred to as Sandmats; some sources list the genus as *Chamaesyce*. *E. humistrata* is sometimes considered a synonym for *E. maculata*, while others consider it a separate species that is difficult to separate from *E. maculata*.

COMPARE: Prostrate Knotweed (*Polygonum aviculare*; non-native) is common throughout our area. Its stems are hairless and the leaf nodes are wrapped with a **papery sheath** (called an ocrea). Leaves, which grow **alternately**, are up to **1 inch** long with **smooth** edges. Flowers have no petals or petal-like projections. Prostrate Knotweed does not produce milky sap when broken. • Leaves and stems of Common Purslane (pg. 46) are more **fleshy**; it does not produce milky sap.

Spotted Spurge   Prostrate Knotweed

GETTING RID OF IT!

The two Spurges described here have small taproots and are fairly easy to pull when the soil is moist. Young Prostrate Knotweed can be hoed or pulled; mature plants are more difficult to remove. Spurge and Prostrate Knotweed plants reproduce by seed, so the best control is to maintain healthy growth of desirable species which will leave no holes for these mat-forming plants to fill.

WHAT'S IT GOOD FOR?

Bees and small insects feed on Spurge flowers, and some birds eat the seeds. The sap makes the foliage bitter, so Spurge is not eaten by most mammals. Some sources report medicinal uses for the foliage or sap.

Carpetweed

(Mollugo verticillata)

OVERVIEW: This non-native annual sprawls along the ground and can form **extensive mats**. **Very thin stems** up to 18 inches long branch out from the central root, and each stem may branch repeatedly; individual mats appear roughly circular. Stem ends may rise several inches above the ground, but Carpetweed is generally **ground-hugging**.

WHERE YOU'LL FIND IT: Carpetweed prefers sunny sites. It thrives in sandy or poor soil, and is common in urban areas where it often sprouts from cracks in pavement. Carpetweed inhabits vacant lots, and is also found in lawns and gardens. It is a pest in the eastern half of our area, and is uncommon in western Minnesota, the Dakotas and northwestern Iowa.

LEAVES: The smooth, hairless leaves are elliptic to narrowly teardrop-shaped, with a rounded or slightly pointed tip and a **pronounced, deep midvein**. They are up to 1¼ inches long, and grow in **whorls** of 3 to 8 leaves (typically 5 or 6); the whorls are spaced fairly far apart along the stems. Leaf bases are typically **swollen at the nodes**.

FLOWERS/FRUIT: Tiny flowers, about ¼ inch across, grow on thin stemlets from the leaf whorls; each whorl may have up to 6 flowers. Five white petal-like sepals surround the green ovary in the center; 3 to 5 white stamens also grow around the ovary. **Faint lines** encircle the edge of the sepals and also run from the tip to the base. Three-part egg-shaped seed capsules replace the flowers.

SEASON: Carpetweed appears from late spring to early summer; flowers are present from midsummer into fall.

OTHER NAMES: Indian Chickweed, Whorled Chickweed, Devil's Grip.

COMPARE: Cleavers (pg. 76) have similar whorled leaves, but have **thicker stems** and are larger, **more erect** plants. • Mats of low-growing Spurges (pg. 28) appear similar at a quick glance, but a closer look reveals that the Spurges have **opposite** rather than whorled leaves. • Purslane (pg. 46) has **thick, fleshy stems** and **thick leaves**.

GETTING RID OF IT!

Carpetweed spreads by seeds, and grows vigorously throughout the season; it can easily take hold in newly seeded lawns. Plants can be pulled when soil is moist, but repeated pulling is necessary to eradicate a colony of Carpetweed. Pre-emergence herbicides will not control it; if chemicals are used, look for one that lists Carpetweed as a target, and apply it when the leaves are present but before the flowers appear. Boiling water may be effective on Carpetweed growing in pavement cracks.

WHAT'S IT GOOD FOR?

Although they are small, the leaves are edible when cooked. Bees and other insects visit the flowers, and some birds reportedly eat the seeds.

White Clover

(Trifolium repens)

OVERVIEW: A common lawn invader, White Clover is a low-growing non-native perennial that is typically **3 to 6 inches** in height.

WHERE YOU'LL FIND IT: Lawns, gardens, parks, roadsides, pastures. Found throughout our region, although it is less reported in South Dakota.

LEAVES: Three-part compound leaves (trifoliate) grow alternately on long stalks. Leaflets are up to ¾ inch long and roughly egg-shaped with tapered bases; edges have **very fine teeth**. Most leaflets have a **whitish V-shape** (called a chevron) that points to the tip of the leaflet. A pair of stipules (leaflike appendages) are present at the base of the stalks, but these are small and easy to overlook.

FLOWERS/FRUIT: Each globe-shaped flowerhead is ½ to ¾ inch across and contains **dozens of tiny white to pinkish-white** flowers that have a larger upward-pointing central petal, with smaller petals and a keel at the base. Flowerheads grow on long, leafless stalks that rise an inch or more above the leaves. Flowers are replaced by small brown seedpods.

SEASON: Spring through fall.

OTHER NAMES: Dutch Clover.

COMPARE: Two similar Clovers are found in our area; they are non-native perennials. • Flowerheads of Red Clover (*T. pratense*) are up to **1 inch** across, with **purplish-red** flowers. Leaflets are up to **1½ inches long** and **elliptic**. Edges may be smooth or very finely toothed, and a white chevron is typically present. One to 3 small **leaflets grow at the base of each flowerhead**. Stipules are **narrow** and up to ½ inch long with distinct veins that may be purplish. Red Clover is up to **3 feet** in height. • Alsike Clover (*T. hybridum*) is up to 2 feet in height. Flowerheads are up to ¾ inch across, composed of whitish to pinkish flowers that become **deep rose-pink** with maturity, starting at the base. Leaflets are up to 1 inch long and have **no chevron**. The stipules are up to **¾ inch long** with a **broad base** and greenish veins.

Alsike Clover

Red Clover

White Clover

GETTING RID OF IT!

Stems of White Clover typically sprawl along the ground and can root at the nodes, forming tough-to-control mats. Small patches can be dug out, if you take care to remove all rootlets. Mow frequently to eliminate flowers before they produce seeds, and pull any remaining leaves and stems when the ground is soft. If chemicals are used to eliminate White Clover in lawns, choose one that's safe for the specific type of grass present.

WHAT'S IT GOOD FOR?

Clovers were introduced as a forage crop for livestock and poultry, and are also used as a cover crop to improve nitrogen levels and stabilize soil banks. Flowerheads are used, fresh or dried, to make herbal tea.

Common Cinquefoil

(Potentilla simplex)

OVERVIEW: This native perennial is a sprawling plant that spreads by **long surface runners** (called stolons) that root at the tips. Runners and stems are slender and green, becoming red with age; they may be smooth or slightly hairy. Plants are typically **low to the ground**, but some stems may rise above a foot or so above the ground.

WHERE YOU'LL FIND IT: Common Cinquefoil is not fussy about habitat; it grows in sun or part shade and tolerates moist or dry areas. It is common in lawns and parks, but also grows in old fields, prairies, meadows and open woods. In our area, it is common in the eastern half.

LEAVES: Compound leaves with 5 leaflets grow alternately on long stalks at fairly wide intervals along the stolons and stems. Leaflets are narrowly teardrop-shaped and up to 1 inch long, with **coarse, rounded teeth** around the edges except at the base, which is narrow and tapered. The undersides of the leaflets are **green**.

FLOWERS/FRUIT: Bright yellow, 5-petaled flowers are up to ½ inch across, with a slightly flattened center; flowers grow **singly** on long stemlets that originate in leaf axils. The petals are **heart-shaped**, typically with a notched tip; the pointed green sepals at the base are **shorter than the petals**. The sepals fold inward to protect the seeds that develop in the center.

SEASON: Common Cinquefoil blooms from spring through midsummer.

OTHER NAMES: Oldfield Cinquefoil, Old-Field Five-Fingers.

COMPARE: Silver Cinquefoil (*P. argentea*) has similar flowers and 5-part compound leaves, but the leaves have several **rounded lobes** in the upper half rather than coarse teeth. Leaf undersides are covered with dense hairs that give them a **silvery** appearance. The sepals are typically the **same length** as the petals. It is up to 1½ feet tall, but sprawls occasionally. In our area, it is found primarily in the northern half, with the exception of the Dakotas and southwestern Minnesota.

Common Cinquefoil

Silver Cinquefoil (2 above, and right)

GETTING RID OF IT!

Common Cinquefoil can be pulled when the soil is moist, but be sure to follow the stolons to locate additional rooting points.

WHAT'S IT GOOD FOR?

Some sources report that preparations made from the root of Common Cinquefoil can be used as an astringent and an antiseptic.

Common Dandelion *(Taraxacum officinale)*

OVERVIEW: This non-native perennial is one of the most well-known—and despised—lawn pests. It grows as a **basal rosette of leaves with flowers sprouting from the center**; the floral stem is generally less than 8 inches tall, although it can be as high as a foot. All parts of the plant, except the flowers, exude a **milky sap** when crushed or broken.

WHERE YOU'LL FIND IT: Prefers full sun but will tolerate partial shade. Found in lawns, gardens, parks, roadsides, waste ground, construction sites and open woodlands. It grows throughout our region, and, indeed, throughout all of the U.S. except the hotter regions in the South.

LEAVES: Soft green leaves are typically up to 8 inches long and an inch wide, but may grow up to a foot in length and several inches in width on monster specimens. Edges have **deep triangular lobes**, giving the plant its common name (from the French *dent de lion* or lion's tooth). Leaves are smooth to slightly hairy and have a pale midrib which may be purplish, particularly towards the center of the plant.

FLOWERS/FRUIT: Bright yellow flowerheads, typically about an inch across, grow singly on a **leafless, tubular stalk** from the center of the plant; the stalk is typically green but may be reddish-purple. The flowerhead consists of strap-shaped disk florets that radiate outward; numerous thin styles arise from the center. Dry **brownish** or greenish-brown seeds, each with a fluffy white tuft of hair, replace the flowers.

SEASON: Dandelions flower continuously from spring through early fall.

OTHER NAMES: *T. vulgare*.

COMPARE: Numerous plants have flowers with a similar appearance. Examples include Sowthistles (pg. 136), Prickly Lettuce (pg. 138) and Meadow Hawkweed (pg. 146). • Red-Seeded Dandelion (*T. erythrospermum*) looks almost identical to the Common Dandelion, but the flowers are typically a bit smaller and the seeds attached to the fluffy tufts are **reddish**. It is scattered throughout our area but uncommon.

GETTING RID OF IT!

Dandelions have a deep taproot which must be removed for effective control. Special dandelion-digging tools are available; they work well when used properly. If herbicides are used, they should be applied in early spring or late summer, when plants are actively growing.

WHAT'S IT GOOD FOR?

Dandelion leaves are edible; young leaves are used raw in salads, and more mature leaves can be cooked. The leaves are quite high in vitamins. Flowers are used to make wine. The roots can be roasted and ground to make a coffee substitute; they can also be peeled, then steamed, to use as a root vegetable (a very labor-intensive process, unfortunately).

Mock Strawberry
(Potentilla indica)

OVERVIEW: Originally from India and other parts of southern Asia, Mock Strawberry is often planted as an ornamental ground cover and has escaped cultivation to become a pest in many areas. It is a low-growing perennial that creeps in vine-like fashion and roots at stem nodes, forming large, mat-like colonies.

WHERE YOU'LL FIND IT: Parks, lawns, open woodlands and waste ground; it prefers areas with light shade and good soil. In our region it is found primarily in the southern half; it is particularly common in Indiana.

LEAVES: Three-part compound leaves grow alternately on long, hairy green stalks. The egg-shaped leaflets have **rounded teeth around the entire edge**; they are up to 2 inches in length and two-thirds as wide. Leaflets are rich green, and smooth to somewhat hairy on top.

FLOWERS/FRUIT: Yellow flowers with 5 rounded petals grow upright on **long, hairy stemlets** that arise from leaf axils. Flowers are about ¾ inch across. Green, pointed sepals and wedge-shaped bracts grow at the base of the flower. Each flower is replaced with a **soft, fleshy red globe** about ½ inch across whose surface is covered with **raised red seeds**, resembling the familiar strawberry (but much smaller).

SEASON: Flowers are present from late spring through midsummer; fruits are ripe from midsummer through late summer.

OTHER NAMES: Indian Strawberry (a reference to the plant's origin in India), *Duchesnea indica*.

COMPARE: True wild Strawberries (*Fragaria virginiana* and *F. vesca*) have 3-part compound leaves and red fruits, but their flowers are **white**. Leaflets are up to 2½ inches long, and the lower portion of the leaflets (closest to the stem) is **untoothed**. True wild Strawberry fruits are usually more elongated or **heart-shaped** rather than globe-shaped, and have **dark seeds** on the surface; they generally hang downward. Wild Strawberries are common throughout our area except in the Dakotas.

GETTING RID OF IT!

Mowing will not eliminate this low-growing plant. Pulling works well, as long as the side shoots are also pulled; repeated efforts will be needed.

WHAT'S IT GOOD FOR?

Mock Strawberry fruits are edible but somewhat dry and almost taste-less. They can be used to add lovely color to fruit salads; however, taste a few before using them, as there appears to be some variation in flavor from patch to patch. Some people report a faint watermelon-like taste, while others (including the author) find the taste disagreeable. Leaves can be used to make tea, and the plant is used medicinally in China.

Creeping Jenny   *(Lysimachia nummularia)*

OVERVIEW: Creeping Jenny is a pretty, perennial ground cover imported from Europe and Asia and sold at nurseries in many states. Unfortunately it spreads vigorously and often escapes into natural areas where it forms dense mats that outcompete native vegetation. Its smooth, light green stems branch repeatedly, rooting at the nodes. Creeping Jenny is typically only an inch or two in height but the mats can be many feet across, particularly in damp, shaded areas.

WHERE YOU'LL FIND IT: Shady lawns and gardens, woodland edges and streambanks. It prefers moist areas. In our region, Creeping Jenny is not reported from the Dakotas, and may also be absent from western Minnesota and western Iowa.

LEAVES: Nearly round leaves up to 1 inch across grow oppositely on short stalks. Leaf edges are smooth. The top side of the leaf is bright green, hairless and **slightly glossy**; faint dots may be observed on the surface. Each leaf has a deep central vein, with several indented lateral veins on each side.

FLOWERS/FRUIT: Bright yellow flowers with 5 petals and 5 yellow stamens grow on short stemlets from leaf axils. Petals have **ruffled edges**, and often have small red dots on them. The fruit is a small round capsule about ¼ inch across; however, many plants don't produce fruits.

SEASON: Flowers are present from late spring (in the southern portions of our region, later in the north) through late summer. Creeping Jenny is usually evergreen in the southern part of our region, and may retain greenish leaves through winter in protected spots in the northern part.

OTHER NAMES: Moneywort, Creeping Yellow Loosestrife.

COMPARE: With its large, opposite, semi-glossy round leaves and mat-forming habit, Creeping Jenny doesn't resemble any other weeds in our area.

GETTING RID OF IT!

Creeping Jenny reproduces primarily by spreading rather than by seed. Pulling is effective if all rooting fragments can be removed. Mowing will not control this plant because it is too low to the ground. Herbicides can be effective, but care must be taken to ensure than any herbicide used is safe for wetlands since this plant frequently grows in wet areas.

WHAT'S IT GOOD FOR?

Creeping Jenny is an attractive ground cover, but many gardeners have been unpleasantly surprised when it escapes the area in which it was planted. Bees and other insects visit the flowers.

Black Medick

(Medicago lupulina)

OVERVIEW: Although individual stems may be up to 2½ feet long, Black Medick generally grows as a sprawling, ground-hugging plant that is noticeable primarily because of its tiny but profuse yellow flowers.

WHERE YOU'LL FIND IT: Found in areas with partial to full sun, including lawns, gardens, edges of parking lots and alleys, roadsides, landscaped areas, pastures and waste ground. This non-native annual is very common throughout our area with the possible exception of South Dakota, where it is likely present but underreported.

LEAVES: Three-part compound leaves grow alternately on hairy stalks that are long at the plant's base, becoming shorter at the top. Leaflets are teardrop-shaped to elliptic with tapered bases and up to ¾ inch long. They are slightly hairy, and have fine teeth along the edges. The central leaflet has a **relatively long stalk**; the 2 side leaflets are sessile.

FLOWERS/FRUIT: Each rounded flowerhead is about **¼ inch across** and contains numerous tiny yellow flowers that have a large central petal, with smaller petals at the base. Flowerheads grow on long stalks from leaf axils. Long clusters of brown seedpods replace the flowerheads.

SEASON: Flowers bloom continuously from late spring through early fall. ·

OTHER NAMES: Black Clover, Black Medic, Hop Clover.

COMPARE: Two non-native, annual Clover plants have similar 3-part leaves and yellow flowers; both grow more **upright**, and flowerheads are **up to ½ inch across**. · The central leaflet of Golden Clover (*Trifolium aureum*) has **no stalk**. Plants may be up to **18 inches tall**. In our region, it is found primarily in northeastern Minnesota, northern Wisconsin, and scattered throughout Michigan. · Like Black Medick, the central leaflet of Low Hop Clover (*T. campestre*) has a **noticeable stalk**. Plants are less than a foot high, and are more **bushy** than the others listed here. It is scarce to absent in the Dakotas and the western parts of Minnesota and Iowa, but is fairly common elsewhere in our region.

Golden Clover

Black Medick

Low Hop Clover

Black Medick

Golden Clover

GETTING RID OF IT!

Black Medick has a deep taproot, but it can be pulled when the soil is moist. It frequently grows in compacted soil, so soil aeration will help eliminate it. Mowing won't control Black Medick because it's too short, but mowing can be effective for Golden Clover and Low Hop Clover. The three plants discussed here reproduce by seed, so they should be removed before seeds develop. The presence of any of them may signal low levels of nitrogen; soil amendments may help prevent their regrowth.

WHAT'S IT GOOD FOR?

Black Medick honey is reportedly popular in some areas. Black Medick and Low Hop Clover are sometimes used as livestock forage.

Pineappleweed

(Matricaria discoidea)

OVERVIEW: Pineappleweed is typically 3 to 6 inches high, but reportedly grows as tall as 12 inches. All parts of the plant have a **sweet, faint pineapple-like scent** when crushed. It is a non-native annual weed.

WHERE YOU'LL FIND IT: Dry areas with gravelly soil, roadsides, abandoned lots and along sidewalks. Pineappleweed often grows in large patches in scrubby areas; it can also grow through cracks in concrete. It is found throughout most of our region, although it is sparse to absent in South Dakota and western Iowa.

LEAVES: The **feathery, fern-like** leaves are up to 2 inches long with a smooth texture; individual leaflets **branch frequently from the central leaf stalk**. Leaves grow alternately on the stems.

FLOWERS/FRUIT: These dome-like flowerheads are yellowish-green to yellow, and ¼ to ½ inch across. They consist of tiny tubular disk florets; they **lack ray florets** and look like small daisies that have lost their petals. Each disk floret is replaced by an oblong brown seed that has no tufts or hairs.

SEASON: Seeds begin germinating in early spring. Flowers are present from late spring through fall.

OTHER NAMES: Wild Chamomile, Disc Mayweed, *Matricaria matricarioides*.

COMPARE: Scentless False Mayweed (*Tripleurospermum inodorum*; also listed as *M. perforata*) has similar foliage, but the leaf texture is more thin and thread-like; its flowers have the **white petal-like ray florets** we normally associate with most daisies. Plants are up to **2½ feet tall**. In our area it is found primarily in the far north. • Dog Fennel (pg. 90) also has similar feathery leaves, but they are pinnately compound, with **leaflets growing oppositely on a central leaf stalk**. Like Scentless False Mayweed, the flowers of Dog Fennel have **white ray florets** surrounding the central yellow disk florets. Dog Fennel has a **strong, unpleasant odor** when crushed. It is up to 2 feet tall.

GETTING RID OF IT!

Pineappleweed reproduces by seed, but it has a branching taproot and is difficult to control. It will succumb to weed sprays that target broadleaf plants, but the best cure is to encourage healthy growth of other plants. Because Pineappleweed thrives in dry areas, frequent watering will help discourage this plant from colonizing an area.

WHAT'S IT GOOD FOR?

Fresh or dried flowerheads make an excellent tea when steeped in hot water for about 10 minutes; the flavor is much like tea made from its close relative, chamomile. Pineappleweed has also been used medicinally to treat stomach complaints, sores and other maladies.

Common Purslane

(Portulaca oleracea)

OVERVIEW: This non-native annual is a succulent, with **fleshy leaves** and a **thick, smooth, rounded stem** that is reddish, pinkish-tan or greenish. Multiple branches grow from a central taproot, and each branch forks repeatedly. It typically hugs the ground, but it may recline against nearby rocks or other structures. It can form mats several feet across.

WHERE YOU'LL FIND IT: Sunny, warm areas with landscape rock are a favored habitat. Also found in waste areas, alleys, unkempt gardens and scrubby lawns. It can grow from pavement cracks and is common in cities. Common Purslane is quite common throughout Iowa, Illinois and Indiana, and is scattered in the remaining states of our region.

LEAVES: **Thick, teardrop-shaped leaves** are **glossy, smooth** and green; some turn purplish later in the season. Leaf sizes vary quite a bit on the same plant, from just over ¼ inch to nearly 1 inch long. Edges are smooth. Leaves grow alternately, but many are so close together on the stems that they appear opposite or whorled, particularly at stem ends.

FLOWERS/FRUIT: Yellow flowers up to ¼ inch across grow singly or in small clusters from stem ends. Flowers appear on sunny mornings, and typically have 5 petals with heart-shaped tips and multiple yellow stamens. (Nursery-grown specimens may have pink, orange or reddish flowers with more petals.) A small cup-shaped green capsule replaces each flower; the top splits off like a lid to release numerous black seeds.

SEASON: Flowers are present from summer through early fall.

OTHER NAMES: Green Purslane, Little Hogweed, Pursley.

COMPARE: Low-growing Spurges and Prostrate Knotweed (pg. 28) grow in dense mats like Purslane, but all parts of those plants produce milky sap when broken, while Purslane **does not produce sap**. In the large photo at right, a stem of Prostrate Knotweed can be seen creeping in front of the Purslane. • Carpetweed (pg. 30) has whorled leaves and grows in mats, but its stems are **very thin**.

Prostrate Knotweed

GETTING RID OF IT!

Purslane reproduces by seed and vegetatively; broken stems will develop roots and create new plants. Pulling can be effective if no broken stems are left behind. Mulching reduces the spread of Purslane.

WHAT'S IT GOOD FOR?

Purslane is a prime wild edible that is also grown as a food plant. Leaves and tender stem tips are used raw in salads, and can also be sautéed. It is often cooked in curries and stir-fries. Purslane is rich in vitamins A and C, and also has high levels of omega-3 fatty acids, magnesium, iron and calcium. Its taste is similar to spinach and, like spinach, it contains high levels of oxalic acid, which may cause problems if over-consumed.

Violets

(Viola spp.)*

OVERVIEW: More than two dozen violet species are found in our region. Most are native, but some are from Europe or Asia. Many violets are ground-hugging plants, but some, including Canada and Downy Yellow Violets, have stems well over a foot long. Often planted as an ornamental for their attractive flowers and foliage, violets are considered weedy when they appear in lawns and other areas where they are not wanted.

WHERE YOU'LL FIND IT: Violets thrive in shady, moist areas, but some may also grow in sunny spots. They spread readily and, if left unchecked, can quickly overtake lawns and gardens. At least one type is present in every state in our region.

LEAVES: Violets have **basal leaves** with floral stems arising from the leaf cluster; some species also have leaves on the floral stems. Many violet species have heart-shaped leaves, but others have oval, circular, lance-like or arrowhead-shaped leaves; several have palmately lobed leaves.

FLOWERS/FRUIT: Flowers have **5 petals, with 2 at the top, 2 facing sideways and 1 at the bottom**. Fruit is a capsule. • Common Blue Violet (*V. sororia*) produces one to several **leafless stems**, each topped with a flower that is usually medium to deep purple but may be white; the throat (base of the petals) is **pale yellowish** at the center, fading to white towards the outside. Petals have purple veins that are strongest on the lower petal; the two side petals are **bearded**, with tufts of **white hair**. • Canada Violet (*V. canadensis*) has both basal and **stem leaves**. Short stems arise from leaf axils, each topped by a white flower with a **dark yellow** throat. The lower petal has several **dark purple stripes** radiating from the throat; fainter stripes appear on the side petals. The back sides of the petals are **pale purple**. • Like Canada Violet, Downy Yellow Violet (*V. pubescens*) has stem leaves, but its petals are **yellow**.

SEASON: Most violets are in flower from spring through early summer. Foliage remains green through early fall.

COMPARE: Other violets can be identified by leaf shape and flower color.

Canada Violet

Common Blue Violet

Downy Yellow Violet

Canada Violet flower and capsule (right)

GETTING RID OF IT!

Violets are annuals or short-lived perennials; they spread by rhizomes and also by seed. All parts of the rhizome must be removed, so digging with a narrow hand trowel or dandelion fork is more effective than simply pulling out the plants. If you want to use herbicides, spray with a blend containing triclopyr; this is most effective when applied during the springtime blooming period, but late summer to early fall also works well.

WHAT'S IT GOOD FOR?

Violets are a good ground cover in shady areas, and their flowers add beauty. The flowers are often candied to use as a decoration; dried flowers can be added to tea blends. The leaves are edible raw or cooked.

Asiatic Dayflower

(Commelina communis)

OVERVIEW: This non-native annual is a polarizing plant. Some gardeners love it for its bright green foliage and interesting flowers. Others have found it weedy and extremely difficult to remove once it takes hold, and it is considered invasive in many areas. It can stand upright to some extent (particularly the stem ends), but commonly grows in creeping, vine-like fashion. Stems are round and hairless, often with a reddish hue; they are up to 3 feet long and frequently root at the nodes.

WHERE YOU'LL FIND IT: Asiatic Dayflower prefers disturbed areas such as vacant lots, edges of parking lots and alleys, roadsides and along build- ings and fences, but it also invades shaded gardens, woodland edges and parks. In our region, it is most common in the southern half, but its range is increasing and it is also starting to show up in the northern part (the author has seen it extensively in the Minneapolis metro area).

LEAVES: Egg-shaped to lance-like alternate leaves with a pointed tip and rounded base are up to 5 inches long and half as wide; edges are smooth. Leaf bases slightly clasp the stem, and a **whitish sheath extends down the stem** from the leaf base. The midvein is **prominent** and **indented**; top surfaces are deep green and smooth.

FLOWERS/FRUIT: Flowers up to ¾ inch across grow singly from leaf axils on a 1-inch stemlet that is usually concealed by a leaf. **Two large, rounded, bright deep blue petals** grow at the top, while a **smaller white petal** grows below them. Several stamens grow from the center; upper stamens are shorter with **bright yellow tips that look like small butterflies**, while the lower stamens are longer and have dull pad-like tips. Each flower lasts one day. A brown capsule replaces each flower.

SEASON: Flowers are present from summer through early fall.

OTHER NAMES: Common Dayflower, Blue Dayflower, Mouse Flower.

COMPARE: With its striking, deep blue flowers and vine-like growth, Asiatic Dayflower is unlikely to be confused with other plants.

GETTING RID OF IT!

Good luck! Not only does this plant spread when stems root at the nodes, but it produces seeds throughout the summer—and they remain viable for years. Pulling is a constant chore as new shoots pop up; also, the stems tend to break off, leaving the roots in the soil. Mowing will help control this plant, if it's in an area that can be mowed. Asiatic Dayflower is resistant to glyphosate; triclopyr is more effective.

WHAT'S IT GOOD FOR?

Young leaves are edible raw, as are the flowers; both can be used in salads. Older leaves can be cooked. Deer eat the leaves; bees feed on the nectar. Some birds eat the seeds.

Ground Ivy

(Glechoma hederacea)

OVERVIEW: As the first photo at right shows, this non-native perennial has aboveground runners (stolons) that branch repeatedly and root at the nodes, making it an aggressive spreader (and each of the side runners shown will grow and send out more runners that also root). Runners may climb up a retaining wall or other structure, appearing to grow upright, but the plants typically rise only a **few inches above the ground**.

WHERE YOU'LL FIND IT: Shade to partial sun, with moist soil. It is a frequent invader of lawns, gardens, mulched areas and disturbed ground. Ground Ivy is common throughout our area except the Dakotas and the western parts of Minnesota and Iowa, where it is scattered or absent.

LEAVES: Kidney-shaped to nearly round, finely hairy leaves, up to an inch long and half again as wide, grow oppositely on **long stalks** attached to **square-edged** runners that are up to 4 inches long between nodes. Leaf edges are **scalloped**; the top surface is deep green, often with a purplish tinge. **Prominent veins** radiate from the base.

FLOWERS/FRUIT: Ground Ivy flowers are **purplish** and **tubular**, with a **3-lobed lower petal** that extends out about ½ inch; a small, notched petal rises above the base of the large petal. The lower petal has **dark purple markings** in the center. Flowers are replaced by small nutlets.

SEASON: Ground Ivy is present from spring through fall; it is typically in bloom from late spring through early summer.

OTHER NAMES: Creeping Charlie, Gill-over-the-Ground.

COMPARE: Henbit (*Lamium amplexicaule*) is a non-native annual that has similar leaves, but they grow in **tight whorls** around the **red** stem; it looks like the stem is growing through a round leaf. Flowers are **pink** and grow in **whorls** around the stem at the top of the plant. Plants **lack creeping stolons**; they may sprawl but are mostly upright and about 1 foot tall. In our region, Henbit is found primarily in the southeastern portion; it is most abundant in Indiana, Ohio and southern Illinois.

GETTING RID OF IT!

Ground Ivy is notoriously hard to control. Hand removal is a tedious job because there are so many root nodes that must be pulled out. Home-made borax spray is a folk remedy that is generally ineffective and may damage desirable grasses. Chemicals containing triclopyr work best, but repeated applications may be necessary; they are most effective when applied during the late spring blooming period.

WHAT'S IT GOOD FOR?

Ground Ivy is a member of the mint family, and while much stronger than garden mint, it does have some similarities. Fresh or dried leaves can be used for tea, and young leaves can reportedly be added to soup.

Big-Bract Verbena

(Verbena bracteata)

OVERVIEW: Big-Bract Verbena is a weedy native plant with **hairy, many-branched stems** up to 18 inches long that **sprawl out in all directions from the central taproot**, forming **large, loose mats**. Portions of the plant, particularly the flowering tips of the stems, **stand or curl upward** to a height of 2 to 6 inches. It is an annual or a short-lived perennial.

WHERE YOU'LL FIND IT: Once you learn to recognize this plant, you'll notice it frequently in urban areas. It grows through cracks in pavement and is also found in gravelly areas, so you'll see it in alleys, along sidewalks, in parking lots, in weedy boulevards and alongside roads. It is fairly common throughout our area except eastern Indiana and most of Ohio.

LEAVES: Leaves at the base are **opposite,** hairy and up to 3 inches long, with a **large central lobe and 2 smaller side lobes** at the leaf base; the central lobe has numerous coarse teeth or additional smaller lobes, creating a **jagged look**. Towards the top of the plant, the leaves become less hairy and smaller, and lack the side lobes. **Hairy, pointed leaflike bracts** surround the flowers, which grow on a terminal spike.

FLOWERS/FRUIT: Tiny **purplish, pinkish or bluish flowers**, ⅛ inch across and 5-petaled, grow in a **whorl** around the terminal spike. The spike elongates with maturity and may be up to 6 inches long in midsummer. Tiny nutlets develop from the bottom of the spike upwards.

SEASON: Flowers are present from late spring through early fall.

OTHER NAMES: Prostrate Vervain.

COMPARE: Corn Speedwell (*Veronica arvensis*; non-native, annual) lacks the long, sprawling stems at the base. Flowering stems stand upright and are typically a few to 8 inches tall; they grow in colonies. **Alternate, lance-like**, hairy leaves are ¼ inch long. When open, the **4-lobed** purplish flowers, just ⅛ inch wide, are visible if you have a sharp eye; otherwise, this plant looks like a **coarse mat of rough green foliage**. It is common in the eastern half of our region, except for northern Wisconsin.

Big-Bract Verbena

Big-Bract Verbena

Corn Speedwell

GETTING RID OF IT!

Big-Bract Verbena reproduces by seed, so the best control strategy is to hoe or cut it off at ground level before the seeds develop; the remaining taproot, which is difficult to pull out of the pavement cracks it frequently grows from, will die before the next season (for more effective control, pour boiling water over the root to prevent regrowth in the current season). Simple pulling is effective for Corn Speedwell, which also reproduces by seed; the seeds need contact with bare ground, so mulching or growing thick turf will prevent it from regrowing.

WHAT'S IT GOOD FOR?

Big-Bract Verbena and Corn Speedwell are reportedly used medicinally.

Common Ragweed

(Ambrosia artemisiifolia)

OVERVIEW: This native annual is one of the main causes of hayfever and other allergies. It grows as a **heavily branched, very leafy** plant that is typically 1 to 2 feet high but can grow to 3 feet. Stems are green or purplish and usually covered with fine white hairs.

WHERE YOU'LL FIND IT: Common Ragweed thrives in sun but will grow in moderately shady areas; it prefers slightly dry soil. It is found in disturbed areas such as vacant lots, railroad embankments, construction sites and roadsides, but also invades lawns, gardens and landscaped areas. Found throughout our area, it is listed as a noxious weed in Illinois and Michigan.

LEAVES: **Fern-like** leaves that are **doubly or triply lobed** grow oppositely (or nearly so) at the base of the plant, but alternately at the top. Leaf stalks are about an inch long and covered with fine white hairs. Leaves are up to 6 inches long and two-thirds as wide at the base; they taper in overall outline, becoming narrower at the tip. They are **lightly hairy when young**, becoming smoother with maturity.

FLOWERS/FRUIT: **Thick, spikelike racemes** (pg. 17) **of tiny green and yellow flowers** grow at the ends of the upper stems; racemes contain both male and female flowers. Racemes elongate as the plant matures; fine yellow pollen is produced by the male flowers.

SEASON: Flowers develop in early summer to midsummer, and release their pollen in late summer to early fall.

OTHER NAMES: Annual Ragweed, Hay Fever Weed, Wild Tansy.

COMPARE: Western Ragweed (*A. psilostachya*; perennial) is similar in appearance, but its leaves are simpler, with **fewer lobes**; they are **finely hairy overall and appear grayish-green**. Plants are **less bushy** overall. In our region, Western Ragweed is found sporadically in the western part; it is largely absent from Ohio, Indiana, southeastern Michigan and southern Illinois. It is less common in urban areas than Common Ragweed.

GETTING RID OF IT!

Common Ragweed grows from a taproot that can be pulled fairly easily;
Western Ragweed has rhizomes and is more difficult to remove cleanly.
Frequent mowing is effective in controlling Common Ragweed. Some
populations of Ragweed have reportedly become resistant to glyphosate.

WHAT'S IT GOOD FOR?

Leaves of both Ragweeds discussed here are used as food by various
insects; pollen is also consumed by bees. Songbirds and some
gamebirds eat the seeds. From a human standpoint, however, the plant
has no uses other than to cause misery.

Giant Ragweed

(Ambrosia trifida)

OVERVIEW: Here's a plant that will horrify any allergy-sufferer who sees it when it is flowering. This native annual has a sturdy, rough-textured green stem that branches occasionally and can reach **12 feet** in height.

WHERE YOU'LL FIND IT: Giant Ragweed prefers sun but will grow in moderately shady areas; it tolerates both moist and slightly dry soil. It is found in disturbed natural areas such as field margins, riverbanks and woodland path edges, but also grows in urban areas where it can be found in gardens, landscaped areas, parking-lot islands, vacant lots, construction sites and freeway embankments. Found throughout our area (with occasional gaps, where it may be present but underreported), it is listed as a noxious weed in Illinois.

LEAVES: Giant Ragweed's distinctive leaves, plus its height, make it easy to identify. Bright green leaves, up to a foot long and three-quarters as wide, grow oppositely on long stalks. Most leaves have **3 to 5 deeply cut lobes that are oval or elliptic with pointed tips**; smaller leaves towards the top of the plant tend to be 3-lobed, or may be unlobed and elliptic. Leaf surfaces are rough, and edges are finely toothed.

FLOWERS/FRUIT: Thick, spikelike racemes (pg. 17) **of tiny green and yellow flowers** grow at the ends of the upper stems; racemes contain both male and female flowers. The racemes elongate as the plant matures; fine yellow pollen is produced by the male flowers.

SEASON: Flowers develop in early summer to midsummer, and release their pollen in late summer to early fall.

OTHER NAMES: Great Ragweed.

COMPARE: Other than its flowering racemes, Giant Ragweed bears little resemblance to its similarly noxious relative, Common Ragweed (pg. 56).

GETTING RID OF IT!

Giant Ragweed has developed resistance to chemicals, including glyphosate, so hand control is necessary. Remove plants before the flowers are
developed. Cutting off the stalks appears to be better than pulling, which
disturbs the ground and may increase germination of dormant seeds.

WHAT'S IT GOOD FOR?

Honeybees collect the pollen, and some caterpillars and moths munch
on the leaves. Some large mammals browse on the leaves. According to
illinoiswildflowers.info, seeds of Giant Ragweed are hard and unappealing
to most birds. From a human standpoint, Giant Ragweed, like its relative
Common Ragweed, has no uses other than to cause misery.

Western Poison Ivy

(Toxicodendron rydbergii)

OVERVIEW: This is the classic "leaves of three, let it be" plant that causes burning, itching rashes and blisters when touched; even clothing that has brushed against the plants can cause a rash upon contact with skin. Western Poison Ivy is a native perennial that is typically seen as a **low plant** less than a foot tall, but it can also grow to several feet in height. It spreads by rhizomes and can form large colonies.

WHERE YOU'LL FIND IT: Western Poison Ivy prefers partial sun and slightly moist areas such as lake edges, stream banks and swamps, but it can also be found in urban parks, along trails, in fields and in ditches. In our area, it is found in the northern half.

LEAVES: Three-part compound leaves grow on the ends of long, thin stalks attached alternately to the main stem. Stalks may be reddish where they join the leaflets, and the **stalk of the central leaflet is longer** than those of the two side leaflets. The egg-shaped leaflets are 2 to 4 inches long, with **irregular toothy or wavy edges**; shallow lobes are sometimes present. Leaflets turn **red** in fall.

FLOWERS/FRUIT: Flowers grow in small clusters in leaf axils. Each is about $1/16$ inch across and has 5 greenish-white triangular petals and 5 yellow-tipped stamens. The **round, ridged berries** that follow are greenish when immature, ripening to **white or whitish-yellow**. Berries grow in upright clusters, and are about $3/16$ inch across; many plants have no berries but must be avoided nonetheless. The berries are toxic.

SEASON: Western Poison Ivy is in flower from early summer to mid-summer. Berries are present starting in late summer; they may persist on the plants through winter.

OTHER NAMES: *Rhus radicans*.

COMPARE: Eastern Poison Ivy (pg. 174) has similar leaves, but typically grows as a **woody vine** that can be up to 60 feet long and uses **aerial roots** to attach itself to trees and supporting structures.

GETTING RID OF IT!

Never burn Poison Ivy, as the smoke causes severe respiratory distress. Wear gloves, long sleeves and pants when dealing with Poison Ivy. Pull or dig out the plants, transferring them to plastic bags for disposal (do not compost). Rinse tools with water, then wash with rubbing alcohol. It may take a few years to kill the plants; glyphosate may be a quicker solution.

WHAT'S IT GOOD FOR?

Native peoples reportedly use Poison Ivy as a dye, and it has also been used medicinally. Some people have no reaction to the compound (called urushiol) that causes the painful reaction, but it is reported that individual sensitivity may develop over time.

Lambsquarters

(Chenopodium album)

OVERVIEW: This annual is generally regarded as native to this region, although some members of its genus were introduced from Europe. It is a leafy plant that is typically 2 to 4 feet tall, although it can grow to 6 feet in good conditions. Its grooved stems are **bluish-green**, often with **reddish stripes**; they are finely hairy when young. It typically branches several times; the side branches become shorter towards the top of the stem, causing an overall pyramidal appearance.

WHERE YOU'LL FIND IT: Sunny, somewhat dry areas with good soil, including gardens, vacant lots, unkempt landscaped areas and old fields. It is found in every state of our region, although it is apparently rare in Iowa.

LEAVES: Alternate leaves up to 4 inches long grow on long stalks; the central vein is prominent, and nodes are often **purplish**. Most leaves are **wedge-shaped**, with **very coarse teeth** on the margins and straight bases that taper towards the stalk in a V-shape; the smallest leaves are linear and may lack teeth. Top sides are green; smaller leaves in the center of the plant have a **white, mealy coating**. Undersides may be fairly smooth on larger leaves, but are whitish and mealy on young leaves. Leaves with the mealy coating will **shed water**.

FLOWERS/FRUIT: Tiny green flowers grow densely packed on a long spike at the end of the main stem and on shorter spikes arising from leaf axils. Flowers are replaced by tiny seeds that are black when ripe.

SEASON: Plants appear in late spring, flowering from early summer to fall.

OTHER NAMES: Goosefoot, Fat Hen, Lamb's-Quarters, Wild Spinach, Pigweed (a name that is also used for various Amaranths; see pg. 66).

COMPARE: Rough Pigweed (pg. 66) and other Amaranths can appear somewhat similar to Lambsquarters, but leaf edges tend to appear **wavy** and **lack the coarse teeth**. Leaves **do not have the mealy coating** found on Lambsquarters.

GETTING RID OF IT!

The best strategy for dealing with Lambsquarters is to pick the young leaves and eat them (see below), then continue picking new growth to eat until the plants are killed by frost. If it is growing in a spot where it can't be tolerated, it is easy to pull.

WHAT'S IT GOOD FOR?

Lambsquarters was called one of the "most nutritious foods in the world" by writer Michael Pollan, and it is well known to foragers across the U.S. Young leaves can be steamed, sautéed or boiled; if the mealy coating is heavy, it can be rubbed off prior to preparation. The ripe, black seeds are also edible, and are favored by savvy foragers as well as by many birds.

Stinging Nettle

(Urtica dioica)

OVERVIEW: This perennial is native to the U.S., although some European subspecies have been introduced in other parts of the country. It may grow to 8 feet tall but is usually shorter. Stems are unbranched; they are **square** with distinct **grooves**, and typically peppered with **short, stinging hairs**. When touched, all parts of the plant cause a **painful burning sensation** that lasts from an hour to a day or more.

WHERE YOU'LL FIND IT: Gardens, landscaped areas, woodland edges, parks and meadows. It grows in both sunny and shady areas. It is reported throughout our region except the southern parts of Illinois and Indiana, and parts of eastern and central South Dakota.

LEAVES: **Elliptic** leaves with narrow, pointed tips grow **oppositely** on half-inch stalks; leaf bases may be tapered, rounded or heart-shaped. Leaves are typically 2 to 5 inches long and less than half as wide at the widest point. Edges are **coarsely toothed**. Three to 7 prominent veins are recessed into the top surface, which is rich green and hairless. A pair of small **leaflike extensions** (called stipules) grow at the base of each leaf stalk; additional smaller leaves may also grow in leaf nodes.

FLOWERS/FRUIT: Clusters of tiny green, greenish-yellow or cream-colored flowers grow on thin stemlets that originate in leaf axils; the clusters are **narrow** and may be **several inches long**. The flowers are replaced by flattened green oval seeds that ripen to brown.

SEASON: Plants begin appearing in spring; flowering takes place throughout summer and into early fall.

OTHER NAMES: Great Nettle, Common Nettle, Itch Weed, Burn Weed.

COMPARE: Wood Nettle (*Laportea canadensis*) is a stinging native perennial that is 2 to 4 feet in height. Its leaves are **oval**; they grow **alternately** except at the top of the plant, where they grow oppositely. A woodland plant that seldom appears in gardens, it grows throughout our region except South Dakota and the western two-thirds of North Dakota.

Stipules (right)

GETTING RID OF IT!

Always wear gloves, long pants and long sleeves when working around Stinging Nettle. Plants reproduce by seed and rhizomes. Mowing will prevent flowering but needs to be repeated frequently. Pulling works for small plants whose rhizomes haven't spread too far; repeated pulling will be necessary to eliminate a developed patch. Don't till Nettle, as that will break up the rhizomes, giving them a chance to re-root (which they will).

WHAT'S IT GOOD FOR?

Young nettle leaves, which can be harvested from young plants or the tops of older plants, are a good wild edible; cooking (or dehydrating) removes the stinging compound. Stems are used to produce textiles.

Rough Pigweed

(Amaranthus retroflexus)

OVERVIEW: This non-native annual is typically 1 to 3 feet tall. Its stout, round stems are pale green or reddish, with subtle, pale **vertical stripes**; stems have fine white hairs that create a **rough** texture. The root is **red**.

WHERE YOU'LL FIND IT: Rough Pigweed prefers full sun and moderately dry soil. In urban areas it is found in waste ground such as vacant lots, edges of parking lots, roadsides, next to buildings and in construction sites; it rarely invades gardens or lawns. It is also found in farmyards and croplands. Rough Pigweed is found in all states in our region and is particularly common in Iowa, Illinois and Wisconsin.

LEAVES: Egg-shaped leaves grow alternately on medium-length stalks. The largest are up to 6 inches long and about half as wide. Edges are untoothed and appear **slightly ruffled**. Veins on the underside are **prominent**; the main vein is pale green and the side veins are whitish.

FLOWERS/FRUIT: Tiny **greenish** flowers are densely packed on **stubby, spikelike racemes** (pg. 17) that branch off floral stemlets attached to the main stem (this configuration is called a panicle); smaller panicles also arise from leaf axils. Spikes are **bristly** and **thicker than a pencil**. Flowers are replaced by tiny seeds that ripen to dark brown or black.

SEASON: Rough Pigweed is in flower from late summer through early fall.

OTHER NAMES: Green Pigweed, Red-Root Amaranth, Common Amaranth.

COMPARE: Slender Amaranth (*A. hybridus*; also called Smooth Pigweed) is a non-native annual that is very similar in appearance to Rough Pigweed, but its flower spikes are **thinner than a pencil** and often **longer** than those of Rough Pigweed; plants can be up to **6 feet** tall and stems are more likely to be red. It is uncommon to absent in the northern and western halves of our region. • Spiny Amaranth (*A. spinosus*; non-native, annual) is up to 4 feet tall and has long, slender floral spikes like Slender Amaranth, but it has stiff **¼-inch-long spines** at leaf nodes. In our region, it is found primarily in Indiana and southern Illinois.

GETTING RID OF IT!

Members of the Amaranth genus can be poisonous to livestock if ingested in large quantities. Preemergent herbicides and mulching can be effective in preventing the growth of Amaranth. Dig out growing plants before they produce seeds, taking care to get several inches of the long taproot to prevent it from regrowing. Many Amaranths are becoming resistant to glyphosate so that may not work on established plants.

WHAT'S IT GOOD FOR?

Young leaves can be cooked like spinach. Ripe seeds can be separated from the chaff and used as a grain; they can also be ground and used in baking, or cooked to make cereal mush. Birds enjoy the seeds as well.

Field Pennycress

(Thlaspi arvense)

OVERVIEW: This now-common annual was brought as a food plant to the U.S. from Europe, probably as far back as Colonial times. It is up to 2 feet in height and can be branched or unbranched. The bright green stem is hairless and **ribbed**.

WHERE YOU'LL FIND IT: Sunny locations, including roadsides, gardens, boulevards in urban areas, and open disturbed areas including pastures and fields. It is fairly common throughout our entire region.

LEAVES: Smooth, oblong leaves up to 4 inches long and one-quarter as wide grow alternately. Edges have shallow, blunt teeth, and the leaf tip is softly pointed. Leaves at the bottom of the plant may grow on short stalks or directly from the stem (sessile); they may wither away by the time the flowers bloom. Leaves on the upper two-thirds of the plant **clasp the stem** and the base of each leaf has a pair of **blunt, ear-like lobes** that are **free of the stem**.

FLOWERS/FRUIT: White, 4-petaled flowers, about ⅛ inch across, grow as short **racemes** (pg. 17) at the ends of the stems on the upper part of the plant. The floral stem elongates over the blooming period, and flowers are replaced from the bottom of the stem up by **flat, oval seedpods** that are up to ½ **inch long** and **notched at the tip**; the seedpods grow on thin stemlets that gently curve upward.

SEASON: Field Pennycress blooms early, typically starting in April and going for about a month. Seedpods begin ripening in midsummer.

OTHER NAMES: Frenchweed, Fanweed, Stinkweed.

COMPARE: Hoary Cress (*Lepidium draba*; also called *Cardaria draba* and Whitetop) is similar in appearance, but the plant is more **robust** overall, with **thicker, more dense leaves** and a **larger floral cluster**. It is found primarily in the southern half of our region, where it is uncommon. It is considered an invasive crop pest and is listed as a noxious weed in Iowa and South Dakota.

GETTING RID OF IT!

Field Pennycress has a deep taproot, so a spade should be used to dig out all the roots if removing by hand. Mowing prior to flower formation can help control Field Pennycress. Seeds germinate in both spring and fall, so weeding may need to be repeated.

WHAT'S IT GOOD FOR?

Oil from the seedpods can be used to make biodiesel. Young, tender shoots were apparently cooked and eaten by the Europeans who brought it over to this country; however, even young portions have a bitter flavor and a strong garlic-turnip odor and many grazing animals avoid it for that reason. Seeds have been used medicinally.

Garlic Mustard

(Alliaria petiolata)

OVERVIEW: A non-native biennial that has become highly invasive in the Northeast U.S. and whose range is extending into the Midwest and elsewhere. The first-year plant is a basal rosette of leaves. The second-year plant has a tender 1- to 4-foot stem that is generally unbranched. All parts of the plant **smell like garlic** when crushed.

WHERE YOU'LL FIND IT: Garlic Mustard prefers shade and adequate soil moisture. Found in parks, along fences and roadsides, in alleys, next to paths, in woodland edges and openings, and on waste ground. Garlic Mustard is present in all states of our region, but is far more common in the southeastern portion. It is surprising that Minnesota is the only state in our region that includes it on their list of noxious weeds.

LEAVES: First-year leaves are up to 3 inches long and **kidney- to heart-shaped** with **scalloped edges**. The rosette **stays green throughout winter**. Leaves of second-year plants grow alternately on short stalks; towards the base of the plant, leaves are similar to those in the first-year rosette. At the top, the leaves become smaller and more **triangular**, with **large, blunt teeth**; they may take on a bronze cast.

FLOWERS/FRUIT: White flowers, about ¼ inch across with 4 petals in the shape of a **cross**, grow **tightly bunched** as a short raceme (pg. 17) at the top of the plant. The raceme elongates over the blooming period, and flowers are replaced from the bottom of the stem up by **slender green seedpods**, 1 to 2 inches long, that **curve upward**.

SEASON: Garlic Mustard blooms from spring through early summer, and is often the only short, tender plant with white blooms in spring woodlands. The flowering stalks die back by early summer; leafless stems with brown seedpods remain for months.

OTHER NAMES: Hedge Garlic, *A. officinalis.*

COMPARE: First-year plants resemble Violets (pg. 48) or large Ground Ivy (pg. 52), but have no flowers.

First-year rosette

GETTING RID OF IT!

Hand-pulling is effective from late fall to early spring. Cut second-year plants at ground level before the seedpods develop. Glyphosate can be used on heavy infestations in spring, when desirable plants are dormant.

WHAT'S IT GOOD FOR?

Garlic Mustard was brought to the U.S. as a food plant. Its leaves were a favored food in springtime, when leafy greens were scarce. Young, early-season leaves can be eaten raw or cooked; they also make a very good pesto (simply substitute Garlic Mustard leaves for the basil). The leaves become bitter in hot weather. Flowers are edible raw and can be used to garnish salads.

Common Peppergrass *(Lepidium virginicum)*

OVERVIEW: A native annual or sometimes a biennial, Common Peppergrass is typically 12 to 18 inches tall. The round central stem branches in the upper half; those stems may branch again, giving it a **bushy** look.

WHERE YOU'LL FIND IT: Vacant lots, scrubby boulevards, roadsides, alleys, patchy areas next to buildings and ill-kept lawns or gardens. It can handle full or partial sun, and varying levels of soil moisture and fertility. In our region, it is common in the southeastern two-thirds; it is scarce or absent in much of Minnesota and the Dakotas.

LEAVES: A cluster of deeply lobed basal leaves, up to 3 inches long and one-third as wide, produces a branched stem that bears alternate, narrow leaves that have **several large, blunt teeth or pointed lobes**, particularly towards the leaf tip. The basal leaves wither away as the plant matures, and are typically not seen when the plant is flowering.

FLOWERS/FRUIT: Tiny flowers grow in racemes (pg. 17) above the leaves. Each is about ⅛ inch across, with 4 **white** petals. The racemes elongate over the season; flat, **oval green seedpods** about ⅛ inch wide develop from the flowers starting at the bottom of the stems. The round seedpods have a **notch at the tip**; they begin developing at the bottom of the raceme while the top of the plant is still flowering.

SEASON: Common Peppergrass flowers from spring to late summer.

OTHER NAMES: Virginia Peppergrass, Virginia Pepperweed.

COMPARE: Green-Flowered Peppergrass (*L. densiflorum*) is very similar, but its flowers tend to be **greenish**, with a few **pinkish** flowers at the top. Leaves on the stem are **smooth-edged**, lacking teeth. It is unclear if this is a native or introduced plant. In our region, it is common in the northwestern two-thirds; it is far less common in Indiana, Ohio and southern Illinois. • Field Peppergrass (*L. campestre*; non-native) has **fuzzy stems and leaves**; the other plants here have **smooth** leaves. In our region, it is most common in Illinois, Indiana, Ohio and Michigan.

GETTING RID OF IT!

Common Peppergrass reproduces by seed and has a slender taproot with fibrous secondary roots. Pulling is effective when soil is moist; always pull plants before the seeds develop, to avoid spreading them.

WHAT'S IT GOOD FOR?

Young leaves are edible raw or cooked, and have a peppery flavor, giving the plant its common name. Green seedpods can be used as a peppery condiment, or mixed sparingly into salads. Dried seeds can be ground and used as a pepper substitute.

White Avens

(Geum canadense)

OVERVIEW: A somewhat **gangly looking** plant, this native perennial can be up to 3 feet tall. The round stem branches occasionally; the upper part is **softly hairy** and has thin, branching floral stems with few leaves.

WHERE YOU'LL FIND IT: A wildflower that is commonly found in open, fairly sunny deciduous woods, White Avens can also pop up in gardens, yards, landscaped areas and parks. It is one of a few plants that can grow under Black Walnut trees, which produce a compound called juglone that inhibits growth of many other plants. It is common throughout our area except in the Dakotas, where it is largely absent.

LEAVES: Several types of leaves grow on various parts of this plant. All are light green, with **shallow to deep lobes** and **toothy edges**; leaves appear somewhat **wrinkled**. A basal cluster of compound leaves up to 7 inches long, each with 3 to 7 leaflets, grows in spring. Leaves on the stems are generally compound with 3 leaflets up to 4 inches long; a few simple, 3-lobed maple-like leaves may also be present. Smaller leaves at the base of the floral stems are elliptic, with several shallow lobes.

FLOWERS/FRUIT: **Bright white** flowers, about ½ inch across, have 5 **elongated** petals that are **as long as, or longer than, the green leaflike sepals** below them; flowers grow on thin stemlets up to 3 inches long. Numerous stamens grow in the center. Flowers are replaced with a **globed cluster** of seeds, each with dry styles that have **hooked tips**.

SEASON: Flowers are present from late spring through early summer.

OTHER NAMES: Canada Avens.

COMPARE: Rough Avens (*G. laciniatum*; native) has white flowers, but the petals are **oval** and **much shorter** than the sepals. Stems are covered with **coarse hairs**. It grows in the eastern half of our region. • Flowers of Yellow Avens (*G. aleppicum*; native) are **yellow**, with **rounded** petals about the same length as the sepals. Leaves have **more prominent** teeth. In our region, it is found primarily in the northern half.

Rough Avens (all 4)

GETTING RID OF IT!

Once it gets into a site with the right conditions, White Avens spreads aggressively, so remove it before it gets out of control. It is easy to pull when the soil is loose; grasp the stem near the ground and pull straight up to get all the roots. If removing a basal cluster, use a sharp-tipped trowel to dig out the roots.

WHAT'S IT GOOD FOR?

Reportedly, the roots can be boiled to use as a chocolate substitute; the author has not tried this curious idea.

Cleavers

(Galium aparine)

OVERVIEW: Numerous members of the *Galium* genus grow in our area. All are short, **weak-stemmed** plants with **whorls of leaves** around the stem; most have fine hairs that **grab onto** clothing, shoes and dogs. Cleavers (*G. aparine*) is by far the most common—and the stickiest.

WHERE YOU'LL FIND IT: Common in open woodlands, Cleavers also grows in gardens, landscaped areas, flowerbeds and along paths and trails. This native annual is found throughout our area, although it is less common (or less reported) in the Dakotas and northern Wisconsin.

LEAVES: Linear leaves with wider tips, 1 to 3 inches long and at most ¼ inch across, grow in whorls of 6 to **8 leaves** that connect directly to the **square, ridged** stem. Like the stems (which are 1 to 3 feet long), leaves are covered with fine, stiff, **downward-facing** hairs that cling to surrounding plants or logs, helping to support the plant.

FLOWERS/FRUIT: Four-petaled white flowers, about ⅛ inch across, grow singly or in small clusters on **very short stemlets** growing from the base of the whorl. A pair of hairy round seedpods replaces each flower.

SEASON: Cleavers bloom from late spring to midsummer.

OTHER NAMES: Catchweed, Sticky-Willy, Bedstraw, Goosegrass.

COMPARE: Fragrant Bedstraw (*G. triflorum*) is a native perennial that has roughly the same range in our area as Cleavers. It is less hairy, and has whorls of 6 **oval** leaves (never 8). Leaves are 2½ inches long or less, and up to **½ inch wide**. Flowers are ³⁄₁₆ inch across and grow on **short stemlets at the ends of long floral stalks** growing from leaf axils or the stem end. Dried leaves **smell like vanilla**. • False Baby's Breath (*G. mollugo*) is an uncommon non-native perennial, found in our area mostly in the counties around the Great Lakes. It has **large, branching clusters of many flowers** at the end of the stems; whorls have 6 or 8 leaves. • Many more *Galium* are found in our area; consult a wildflower book or search "*Galium*" online.

Cleavers   Fragrant Bedstraw

GETTING RID OF IT!

Cleavers and other annual *Galium* spread by seed; Fragrant Bedstraw
and other perennial *Galium* also spread vegetatively. Young plants can
be pulled or hoed before they flower; continue to pull new plants as they
appear and eventually you will reduce or eliminate the plants. Mowing can
help control the spread of plants; aerating will also discourage *Galium*.

WHAT'S IT GOOD FOR?

Young growth, picked before the plants flower, can be boiled or added
to soups; some people eat young leaves raw in salads but many will find
the hairy texture unacceptable. Note that some people experience a mild
rash when they contact the plants, and such people should not eat them.

Cow Parsnip

(Heracleum maximum)

OVERVIEW: This sturdy-looking native perennial is typically 4 to 5 feet tall, but can grow to 8 feet. Its stem is 1 to 2 inches across and typically unbranched. The surface is lightly **ridged**; it is green to purplish and covered with **fine white hairs**. Contact with the plants may irritate skin.

WHERE YOU'LL FIND IT: Although this plant is usually found in meadows, open woodlands and streambanks, it also grows along highways and in ditches near suburbs and towns close to agricultural or natural areas. It grows in all states of our region but is most common in the central area.

LEAVES: Robust, **3-part compound** leaves grow alternately on stalks up to 10 inches long; a partially open **sheath covers the stalk** where it joins the main stem. Leaflets are up to **1 foot long**, with **3 large lobes** that have additional coarse, pointed lobes and jagged teeth.

FLOWERS/FRUIT: **Flat-topped clusters** up to 8 inches wide grow on long stalks at the top of the plant. The large cluster is made up of smaller clusters of ¼-inch white flowers, which are replaced by oval seedpods.

SEASON: Flowers are present from late spring through midsummer.

OTHER NAMES: Hogweed, *H. lanatum.*

COMPARE: Cow Parsnip is often compared to Queen Anne's Lace (pg. 96), which also has large clusters of small white flowers. But leaves of Queen Anne's Lace are **fern-like** and its central stem is **slender**. It is 2 to 4 feet tall. • Wild Parsnip (pg. 114) has similar robust leaves and a large, flat-flowering cluster, but its flowers are **yellow**. • Giant Hogweed (*H. mantegazzianum*) is the king-size version of Cow Parsnip; it may grow to **15 feet tall**. Stems of this non-native perennial are up to **3 inches thick** and **mottled with purple**. Leaves are similar to those of Cow Parsnip, but up to **5 feet** across. Giant Hogweed causes very severe cases of *phytophotodermatitis* (see pg. 114 for more information on this). This plant is uncommon in our region; it is found occasionally in Minnesota, Wisconsin, Michigan, Illinois, Indiana and Ohio.

GETTING RID OF IT!

Cow Parsnip reproduces by seed and develops a large taproot. The taproot and any root clusters should be dug out with a spade. The plant contains a chemical that *may* cause blisters or skin irritation; see pg. 114 for more information. The reaction, when it occurs, is not as severe as that caused by Wild Parsnip or Giant Hogweed, but gloves, long pants and long sleeves should be worn when removing Cow Parsnip.

WHAT'S IT GOOD FOR?

Many insects collect pollen and nectar from the large flower clusters. Early Native peoples peeled young stems and cooked them as a vegetable; or used them to make soup.

Shepherd's Purse

(Capsella bursa-pastoris)

OVERVIEW: A scraggly-looking plant that would go unnoticed except for its white flowers and oddly shaped seedpods that grow on **long, thin stems**. This non-native annual has a flowering stem up to 2 feet in height, although it is usually shorter than that. Stems are often erect, but may sprawl sideways; plants may have numerous stems.

WHERE YOU'LL FIND IT: Full to partial sun; it thrives in areas that may be too dry to support many other plants. It readily populates disturbed areas, and is found in gardens and patchy lawns, next to buildings, along alleys, in unkempt landscaped areas, along roads, in playground areas and ball fields, and sunny fields and pastures. It is quite common throughout our region, although it is less reported in South Dakota.

LEAVES: The **basal cluster of lobed, lance-like leaves** can be up to 9 inches across, although it is typically smaller. Leaves are 2 to 4 inches long and one-quarter as wide; lobes are triangular or have rounded tips. A few small elliptic leaves grow alternately on the flowering stem.

FLOWERS/FRUIT: Tiny flowers grow as a small raceme (pg. 17) at the tops of the stems. Each is about ¼ inch across, with 4 white petals; flowers are very short-lived. The racemes elongate over the season; flat, somewhat **heart-shaped green seedpods** about ¼ inch long develop from the flowers starting at the bottom of the stems. Seedpods develop at the bottom of the raceme while the top of the plant is still flowering.

SEASON: Flowers are present from late spring through late summer.

OTHER NAMES: *Bursa-pastoris* means "purse of the shepherd" in Latin. This plant seems to have no other common names.

COMPARE: At a very quick glance, Common Peppergrass (pg. 72) might be mistaken for Shepherd's Purse, but it lacks the basal cluster. Its racemes have **many more seedpods** on them, and they grow more **closely together**; its seedpods are **round with a notched tip**.

GETTING RID OF IT!

If you have Shepherd's Purse growing in your lawn, that is a sign that your turfgrass is not healthy. Improved cultural practices, coupled with frequent mowing, will eventually force out Shepherd's Purse. With its slender taproot, Shepherd's Purse is fairly easy to pull from other areas when the soil is moist.

WHAT'S IT GOOD FOR?

Seedpods and leaves can be eaten raw or cooked; they have a peppery, spicy flavor. All parts of the plant provide a food source to various insects, birds and mammals.

Hoary Alyssum

(Berteroa incana)

OVERVIEW: Stems of this non-native perennial can reach 2 feet or more in length. It may stand upright to show off its lovely little flowers, but it often sprawls in a messy heap.

WHERE YOU'LL FIND IT: Alleys and boulevards, meadows and prairies, dry degraded areas, patchy lawns, edges of railroad tracks, paths, pastures and landscaped areas. Quite common in the northern half of our region, it is listed as a noxious weed in Michigan and was formerly on Minnesota's noxious weeds list.

LEAVES: A basal cluster of lance-like to elliptic leaves appears in spring from seeds that have germinated the previous fall. By the time the plant is in flower, the basal cluster is gone. The lower part of the stem is typically unbranched, and has numerous alternate leaves up to 3 inches long that are elliptic with softly pointed ends; the leaves are attached directly to the stem (sessile). Leaves on the upper branched stems are smaller. Both leaves and stems are covered in fine hairs, which produce a **grayish-green hue**.

FLOWERS/FRUIT: Flowers grow in **rounded clusters** on floral stems at the tops of the branching stems. Each flower is about ¼ inch across, with 4 white petals that are so **deeply cleft** they give the appearance of 8 petals. The stems elongate over the season; **flat, disc-like green seedpods** develop from the flowers starting at the bottom of the stems and are present while the top of the plant is still flowering. The seedpods are **¼ inch long**; they **point upward** and have a **short, spikelike style** at the end.

SEASON: In bloom from late spring through fall.

OTHER NAMES: Hoary False Madwort.

COMPARE: The flowers are very similar to those of Chickweeds (pg. 26), but the leaves of Chickweeds grow oppositely and most varieties are much shorter in stature than Hoary Alyssum.

GETTING RID OF IT!

Prairies are sometimes burned to control this plant, which outcompetes native plants and provides poor forage for grazing animals. In home settings, hand-pulling can be effective if the taproot can be extracted; this may require a shovel, as the taproot can become fairly long.

WHAT'S IT GOOD FOR?

Bees and other insects visit the flowers. Unfortunately, Hoary Alyssum is known to cause illness in horses that eat the plants, and it doesn't seem to have any uses for people other than for those who wish to enjoy its abundant clusters of tiny flowers.

Horse Nettle

(Solanum carolinense)

OVERVIEW: This vicious weed is a native perennial that is much hated by farmers and gardeners alike. Stems are typically about 2 feet tall, although they can grow to 3 feet. They are **hairy** and well armed with **sharp yellow spines** that can stick in the skin and break off.

WHERE YOU'LL FIND IT: Horse Nettle is at home in sunny areas, and can be found in agricultural areas as well as suburban and rural gardens. It also grows along railroad embankments, fences and trails, and in waste ground in both rural and urban areas. In our region, it is primarily found in the southern half, where it is very well established; it is not currently reported from North Dakota. It is listed as a noxious weed in Iowa.

LEAVES: Appearing a bit like a **rounded oak leaf**, Horse Nettle leaves are **irregularly lobed**; they are up to 7 inches long and two-thirds as wide. They grow alternately on short stalks. On the underside, the midrib and some of the veins have more of those **sharp, nasty spines**.

FLOWERS/FRUIT: Small clusters of **star-shaped white to pale lavender flowers**, about ¾ inch across with hairy stemlets, grow at the branch tips. The 5 petals are fused at the base; 5 bright yellow stamens appear in the center. **Smooth,** round, many-seeded berries up to ¾ inch in diameter follow; they have a 5-part crown at the top, resembling tiny tomatoes. They are **green with dark stripes** when young, ripening to **yellow or orangish**; they often become wrinkled when mature.

SEASON: Flowers begin appearing in late spring or early summer, and continue to bloom all summer. Fruits develop a week or two later, and can be found through early fall.

OTHER NAMES: Carolina Horse Nettle.

COMPARE: Buffalo Bur Nightshade (*S. rostratum*) is similar, but its leaves are more **deeply lobed**. Flowers are **bright yellow** and slightly larger, and its fruits are **covered in spines**. In our region, it is found primarily in Illinois, Indiana, and the southern parts of Minnesota and Wisconsin.

Horse Nettle

Horse Nettle

Buffalo Bur
(above and right)

GETTING RID OF IT!

Horse Nettle spreads by roots and by seed. Deep hoeing or careful digging is the best way to attack this plant. The roots are very deep, and you'll need to dig out several inches. Root fragments can make new plants, so be sure to dispose of them where they can't regrow.

WHAT'S IT GOOD FOR?

Bees collect pollen from the flowers, and some animals and birds eat the ripe fruit. Green berries are mildly toxic to humans, and even ripe berries are reported to be toxic in large quantities. When enough is eaten, all parts of the plant except the mature fruit can be toxic to livestock, who rarely browse it in quantity because of the spines.

White Campion

(Silene latifolia)

OVERVIEW: Although it's considered a weedy pest, this non-native plant provides an interesting look at plant biology. It is dioecious, meaning flowers are either male or female; and when the female flower has been fertilized, the base of the flower (called the "bladder" in this case) grows noticeably fatter. White Campion is typically 2 to 3 feet tall, with **finely hairy** round stems; several stems may grow from the same taproot. It is an annual or short-lived perennial.

WHERE YOU'LL FIND IT: Disturbed ground and waste places with sun to part shade are common locations, but it also grows in gardens, parklands and woodlands, particularly along edges and paths. It is common in the northern two-thirds of our region with the exception of the Dakotas and western Iowa, where it seems to be scarce or absent.

LEAVES: The opposite leaves are **lance-like and finely hairy** on both surfaces, with untoothed edges. Those at the base are up to 5 inches long and grow on a short stalk. Leaves become smaller towards the top and are attached directly to the stem. Leaf nodes are swollen.

FLOWERS/FRUIT: White flowers up to **1½ inches long** grow at the top of the stem, singly or in loose clusters; they have 5 white, notched petals. The bladder at the base is **hairy**; it is generally greenish, but may be **streaked with maroon** on male flowers. The flower structure is different for male and female flowers; please see the photos at right. The fruit is a brown, urn-like capsule that opens at the top to release seeds.

SEASON: White Campion flowers from early to late summer.

OTHER NAMES: Evening Campion, Evening Lychnis, White Cockle, Catchfly.

COMPARE: Two non-native Campions below are less common. **Leaves and bladders of both are hairless**, flowers grow in **clusters**, and stems are **waxy**. • Balkan Catchfly (*S. csereii*) has **widely oval** leaves that **clasp the stem**. Its bladders are **narrow**. • Bladder Campion (*S. vulgaris*) has **lance-like** leaves. Its bladders are **fat** and **distinctly veined**.

Balkan Catchfly

White Campion
Female flower (top circle),
Male flower (bottom circle)

Bladder Campion

GETTING RID OF IT!

White Campion has a sturdy root system, but can be pulled when plants
are small. It reproduces by seed, so plants should be removed before
flowering, which continues for several months. Larger plants can be cut
with a hoe, then a few inches of the taproot should be dug out to prevent
regrowth; the hole should covered with fresh dirt. Some herbicides,
including 2, 4-D, are not effective on White Campion; hand control is best
for the home gardener.

WHAT'S IT GOOD FOR?

The flowers are attractive to some moths, but this plant is not a favorite
of wildlife. It does not seem to have any medicinal uses.

Yarrow

(Achillea millefolium)

OVERVIEW: A member of the Aster family, Yarrow is a perennial that is typically 1 to 2 feet tall. The stem is green and is typically lightly fuzzy; it branches into several floral stems at the top. Yarrow spreads easily and may grow in colonies. It is generally considered to be a native plant, but there is a non-native variety that may also be present.

WHERE YOU'LL FIND IT: Yarrow grows in full sun or partial shade, and prefers moderate soil moisture. It is typically found in natural areas such as open woods, fields and prairies, but also appears in yards and garden edges, along roadsides and in office park shelterbelts. It is very common throughout our region.

LEAVES: Very **feathery, fern-like** leaves grow alternately; the leafstalks have **fine, soft multi-branched leaflets** growing closely packed from the tip to the leaf base. Leaves are light to bright green, and may be sparsely arranged on the stem or fairly close together. Those at the bottom of the plant are up to 6 inches long and 1 inch wide; they become smaller towards the top of the stem.

FLOWERS/FRUIT: **Flat-topped to slightly rounded clusters** (corymbs), 2 to 4 inches wide, grow at the ends of the main stem and branching stems. Individual flowers are white or, occasionally, pale pink, and about ¼ inch across. They have 5 rounded petals with notched tips; the central disk is **yellowish**. Before the flowers open, the cluster looks like a **tiny, fuzzy head of cauliflower**. Flowers are replaced by oval, somewhat prickly-looking seedheads that are brown when mature.

SEASON: Yarrow is in bloom from early summer to early fall.

OTHER NAMES: Common Yarrow; in the Southwest it is called *plumajillo* ("little feather" in Spanish).

COMPARE: Yarrow bears a vague resemblance to Queen Anne's Lace (pg. 96), but Queen Anne's Lace leaves are more **fern-like** than feathery, and Yarrow is a simpler, shorter, less branched plant.

GETTING RID OF IT!

Yarrow is often planted in gardens, but it spreads by seed as well as by rhizomes and can escape to areas where it is not wanted. Small plants can be successfully pulled if the soil is moist; larger plants will require digging, taking care to get all of the rhizomes. Triclopyr is an effective chemical control that is less dangerous than glyphosate.

WHAT'S IT GOOD FOR?

Yarrow is used medicinally; according to the website botanical.com, it was used in Sweden to make beer. Bees, flies and wasps collect nectar and pollen from the flowers. The foliage is bitter and is avoided by most browsing animals.

Oxeye Daisy

(Leucanthemum vulgare)

OVERVIEW: With its cheerful blooms, Oxeye Daisy may appear to be a desirable plant. But this non-native perennial forms dense colonies and spreads rampantly; it is considered an increasing threat to native vegetation. The stem is slightly angled and green, sometimes with thin burgundy stripes; it is typically **unbranched** and 1 to 3 feet tall.

WHERE YOU'LL FIND IT: Oxeye Daisy is not particular about its habitat preferences, and seems to thrive just about anywhere: lawns, gardens (where it is sometimes deliberately planted), boulevards, roadsides, parks, prairies, vacant lots . . . the list goes on. It is common throughout our region except the Dakotas and southwestern Minnesota, where it is uncommon. Ohio lists it as a state-level noxious weed.

LEAVES: Oblong leaves with a broad leaf stalk grow in a small basal cluster, and also alternately on the lower part of the stem; these leaves appear **spoon-shaped** and are up to 5 inches long, with **coarsely toothy or roundly lobed** edges. Leaves become smaller as they ascend the stem. At the stem top, leaves are widely spaced and an inch or so long; they have no stalks and are **linear** with broad teeth or narrow lobes.

FLOWERS/FRUIT: This is the **classic daisy**, with **15 to 35** petal-like white ray florets and a **flattened** central disk composed of tiny, tubular yellow disk florets. Flowers are up to **2 inches** across; they grow singly on top of the stems. The disk florets become hard, dry seeds.

SEASON: The blooming period is from early summer to late summer.

OTHER NAMES: Common Daisy, *Chrysanthemum leucanthemum*.

COMPARE: Dog Fennel (*Anthemis cotula*; also called Stinking Chamomile) has similar flowers, but they are only about 1 inch across and have **less than 20** ray florets; the yellow disk becomes **rounded** with maturity. Stems **branch repeatedly**. Leaves are **feathery**, with **multiple, flat** segments. The foliage has a **strong, disagreeable scent**. In our region, this non-native annual is common in the southeastern two-thirds

Oxeye Daisy

Dog Fennel

GETTING RID OF IT!

Oxeye Daisy spreads by seeds and also by rhizomes; it has a fairly deep taproot. Sheep, horses and goats will eat the plants and control their spread, but that isn't practical for most homeowners. Dig the plants out with a narrow spade, going deep enough—about 6 inches—to remove the entire root; broken pieces of rhizome will sprout and produce new plants. Mowing should be done prior to flowering, and will slow, but not stop, the growth of the plants. Mulching can help prevent seed germination.

WHAT'S IT GOOD FOR?

Young leaves are eaten raw in salads; they have a bitter taste similar to arugula. Cut flowers are attractive, and keep well in a vase of water.

Hairy Galinsoga
(Galinsoga quadriradiata)

OVERVIEW: This non-native annual is typically about a foot tall, but stems range from less than 6 inches to 2½ feet long; longer stems may sprawl along the ground. Stems are **densely hairy**. Hairy Galinsoga spreads by seeds and is very prolific. Some gardeners have gotten an infestation of Hairy Galinsoga from compost or potting mix.

WHERE YOU'LL FIND IT: Known as an agricultural weed, Hairy Galinsoga also appears in urban areas, particularly where the ground has been disturbed. It is found in gardens, along roads and alleys and in sparse dirt next to buildings; it can grow from pavement cracks. It prefers sun or partial shade. Although present in every state of our region, it is most common east of the Mississippi River, particularly southern Wisconsin.

LEAVES: Deep green, egg-shaped, with **coarsely toothed edges**, a pointed tip and rounded base. They grow oppositely and are up to 2½ inches long with **sparse to dense hairs** on the upper surface.

FLOWERS/FRUIT: Flowers are ¼ inch across, and grow at the ends of hairy stemlets. Central disk florets are deep yellow and ringed by stubby white petal-like ray florets. There are 5 ray florets, each with **3 rounded teeth**. Each disk floret is replaced by a dry seed with fluffy hairs.

SEASON: Hairy Galinsoga is in flower from early summer through fall; it is generally killed by frost.

OTHER NAMES: Shaggy Soldier, Peruvian Daisy, Common Quickweed.

COMPARE: Small-Flowered Galinsoga (*G. parviflora*; also known as Lesser Peruvian Daisy) is very similar, but is slightly **less hairy** overall; the **central yellow disk is larger** in proportion to the ray florets, which are tiny and often have only 2 rounded teeth. Its leaves are often paler than those of Hairy Galinsoga, and its **seeds lack the pappus**. It is officially listed as being present in all states of our region except South Dakota, but it is fairly uncommon.

Hairy Galinsoga
(above and left)

Small-Flowered
Galinsoga (right)

GETTING RID OF IT!

Hairy Galinsoga is much hated by farmers because it develops seeds rapidly and continues to flower until the frost; it can reduce crop yields by nearly half, and is host to a number of agricultural diseases. In the home garden, it is essential to pull plants before the seeds develop. Remove pulled plants from the garden area and either discard, or place in a very active, hot compost pile. Continued weeding vigilance is required to prevent an infestation.

WHAT'S IT GOOD FOR?

Its tiny flowers are rather charming, but the plant apparently has little else to recommend it.

Black Nightshade

(Solanum ptycanthum)

OVERVIEW: This native annual has stems that may be up to 3 feet long, although they are usually shorter. Plants branch frequently; they often recline or sprawl sideways. Stems are green, sometimes with a purple tinge; they are rounded or slightly angular, often with scattered hairs.

WHERE YOU'LL FIND IT: Full to partial sun, variable moisture levels. It is common in alleys, gardens, parks, vacant lots and waste ground, but also grows in woodland openings, thickets and rocky areas. It is common throughout our region except the Dakotas, where it is scattered.

LEAVES: Alternate, **slightly hairy** on both surfaces and often **purplish** underneath. They are egg-shaped, with pointed tips and long stalks that are **winged** near the leaf base. Edges may be smooth or wavy, or may have wide, blunt teeth. Leaves are up to 3 inches long and two-thirds as wide; numerous smaller leaves grow along the stem.

FLOWERS/FRUIT: Small clusters of flowers grow on **short stalks that join together** at the end of a ¾-inch stemlet that grows from the main stem or from a leaf axil. Flowers are star-shaped and about ¼ inch across; they have 5 pointed **white** petals that **fold or curl backwards**, away from the **bright yellow** stamens in the center. Fruits are **mottled green** ⅓-inch berries with a **star-shaped cap**; fruits ripen to **black**.

SEASON: Flowers grow throughout summer; berries ripen from mid-summer into early fall.

OTHER NAMES: West Indian Nightshade, Eastern Black Nightshade, *S. ptychanthum*. Some sources list *S. nigrum* as a synonym, but most say it is a non-native species that is not found in our region.

COMPARE: Horse Nettle (pg. 84) has similar leaves and white flowers, but its stems and leaf undersides have **sharp spines**; its ripe fruit is **yellow or orange**. • Bittersweet Nightshade (pg. 186) is related, but it is a **vine** that has **purple** flowers; its fruits are **red** when ripe.

GETTING RID OF IT!

Black Nightshade has a slender, branched taproot. The plant is fairly easy to pull when the ground is moist. It spreads by seeds, so be sure to remove it before the berries form.

WHAT'S IT GOOD FOR?

Although the leaves and unripe fruit are toxic, ripe black berries are edible, but this may vary from area to area; they are recommended only for experienced foragers who are familiar with the plants found locally. Birds, small mammals and deer enjoy the ripe fruits, and bees gather pollen from the flowers. The leaves are bitter, but are frequently peppered with holes that are apparently made by insects feeding on the leaves.

Queen Anne's Lace

(Daucus carota)

OVERVIEW: The distinctive part of this non-native biennial is the second-year flowering plant, which is 2 to 4 feet tall. Its **slender** green stem is **hairy** and has fine vertical lines. It often grows in **large colonies**.

WHERE YOU'LL FIND IT: Sunny, dry areas, including yards, gardens, parks and waste areas, as well as in fields, on railroad embankments and along roads. It is very common in the southeastern two-thirds of our region and is listed as a noxious weed in Iowa, Michigan and Ohio.

LEAVES: The compound, **fern-like** leaves are **sparsely hairy** underneath. The first-year basal cluster is a rosette that **looks like a carrot top**. Leaves of second-year flowering plants grow alternately, attached to a **sheath** that connects to the main stem. Leaflets are divided into additional segments; some segments are **flat, with additional small, flat lobes**, while others are more **feathery**. Lower leaves are twice compound and up to 10 inches long, with **thin, feathery** leaflets.

FLOWERS/FRUIT: Flat-topped floral clusters (umbels), 2 to 5 inches across, grow on leafless stalks from stem ends. The large clusters are made up of smaller clusters of ⅛-inch white flowers. The large cluster often has a few **dark purple flowers in the center**. The stemlets of all clusters join together at the top of the floral stalk. **Long, thin green bracts** grow below the cluster. As they mature, clusters turn brown and curl inward, forming a **bird's-nest shape** that is filled with ribbed seeds.

SEASON: Flowering is continuous from summer through early fall.

OTHER NAMES: Wild Carrot, Chigger Weed.

COMPARE: Poison Hemlock (*Conium maculatum*) has similar flowers, but **lacks the long bracts**. Leaves are also similar but **hairless** underneath. The stem is **thick, hairless** and **dotted with purple**. Plants are 3 to **8 feet** tall. In our area, this **highly toxic** non-native biennial is found mostly in the southern half, where it grows in low areas, fields and roadsides. • Also see Cow Parsnip on pg. 78.

Queen Anne's Lace,
leaf with sheath

Queen Anne's
Lace (above)

Poison Hemlock
(left)

Queen Anne's Lace
(above and right)

GETTING RID OF IT!

Queen Anne's Lace can be pulled when young; as the plants mature they develop a deep taproot that can be difficult to completely remove. New plants will sprout from any root remnants, so it's worth it to try to dig them out with a narrow-bladed spade. Large infestations can be mowed when the plants start flowering, but this may need to be repeated. Whatever you do, don't let the plants go to seed; they will spread wildly. Queen Anne's Lace is known to harbor chiggers, so watch out when weeding!

WHAT'S IT GOOD FOR?

Flowers are used to make jelly; be certain you have picked flowers of Queen Anne's Lace—not deadly Poison Hemlock! Roots of the first-year plant can be cooked like carrots, but are reportedly stringy and tough.

Horseweed

(Conyza canadensis)

OVERVIEW: This native annual can quickly grow to 6 feet in favorable conditions. Stems and leaf edges are covered with **short, stiff hairs**. Multiple floral stems branch out in the upper part of the squarish stem, which may droop or fall over from the weight of the flowering clusters.

WHERE YOU'LL FIND IT: With the exception of a few pockets here and there, this plant is found throughout the entire lower 48 states of the U.S. It prefers full sun, and thrives in disturbed areas including old fields, fencerows and pastures. In urban and suburban areas, it is found in poorly maintained gardens, patchy landscaped areas, scrubby edges of parkland, areas with decorative rock or gravel, empty lots, and along roads and railroad tracks.

LEAVES: Lance-like to linear leaves, typically 2 to 3 inches long, grow alternately, attached directly to the stem (sessile); the tips are sharply pointed. They are **closely spaced** on the stem and become a bit smaller towards the top. The lower leaves have a few wide, shallow teeth; upper leaves have no teeth.

FRUIT/FLOWERS: Numerous flowers grow in **large, branching clusters** (panicles) at the top of the plant. Individual flowerheads are about ³⁄₁₆ inch long and ⅛ inch across, and consist of a bullet- to vase-shaped **green base** packed with **very short white ray florets** that barely reach above the green base; a yellow disk is tucked in the center. Brown seeds with fluffy tufts of light brown hairs replace the flowers.

SEASON: Horseweed begins growing in spring, and flowers from mid-summer to early fall.

OTHER NAMES: Canada Fleabane, *Erigeron canadensis*.

COMPARE: Young Horseweed plants with no flowers resemble Leafy Spurge (pg. 118), Toadflax (pg. 128) or Goldenrod (pg. 142), but once the flowers develop, it is easy to tell them apart. • Pilewort (pg. 110) has similar flowers, but its leaves are much larger and **coarsely toothed**.

GETTING RID OF IT!

Horseweed reproduces by seed, and can quickly take over an area where there is little competition. It is easy to pull, especially when it is still small; look for fuzzy, bright green linear leaves on a furry stem. Like many weeds, Horseweed has become resistant to glyphosate.

WHAT'S IT GOOD FOR?

Native peoples reportedly made tea from Horseweed to use medicinally. Dried leaves can be used as a culinary herb, and young leaves can be cooked as a potherb.

Venice Mallow

(Hibiscus trionum)

OVERVIEW: It's too bad that this non-native annual spreads so easily into areas where it isn't wanted, because its flowers are quite lovely (although they are short-lived, and the foliage isn't particularly interesting). It starts as a simple upright plant, but soon becomes a sprawling monster with vine-like stems up to 2 feet long and 1 foot high. Stems are round, light green and hairy, and branch at the base, extending the sprawling effect.

WHERE YOU'LL FIND IT: Sunny areas with adequate moisture. It is often included in seed mixtures, and has become a pest in urban gardens, where it spreads from its intended home into a neighboring yard. It prefers disturbed areas and is found in vacant lots, in waste areas and along roads and railroad tracks; it also grows in fields, orchards and agricultural areas. In our region, it grows primarily in southeastern Iowa, the northern parts of Illinois and Indiana, the southern parts of Wisconsin and Michigan, and much of Ohio. It is scattered in the Dakotas and southern Minnesota.

LEAVES: **Narrow, 3-part compound leaves** with **rounded lobes** grow alternately on long stalks. The central leaflet is up to **3 inches long**; side leaflets are shorter. Leaflets somewhat resemble dandelion leaves.

FLOWERS/FRUIT: A single white, 5-petaled flower with a **deep purple throat and bright yellow-tipped stamens** grows on a long stemlet that arises from a leaf axil; the flower develops from a distinct **pod-like** bud with **vertical maroon ridges**. Flowers are up to 2½ inches wide; each opens only on a sunny day, and only for a few hours. A 5-part seed capsule replaces each flower.

SEASON: Venice Mallow is in bloom from midsummer to early fall.

OTHER NAMES: Flower-of-an-Hour, Bladder Hibiscus, *Trionum trionum*.

COMPARE: The flowers resemble some domestic *Hibiscus* cultivars, although the buds are quite different in appearance.

GETTING RID OF IT!

Venice Mallow spreads by seed; the seeds can lie dormant in the soil for decades and still be viable. Pulling before seeds develop will remove the current year's crop, but this will need to be repeated annually as dormant seeds sprout. Even if you want to keep the plant around to enjoy its blooms, always cut spent flower heads to prevent it from going to seed.

WHAT'S IT GOOD FOR?

Some people really enjoy the fleeting beauty this flower provides; others can't pull it fast enough. Keep in mind that even if you enjoy it in your garden, seeds travel far and may infest the garden of someone who doesn't want it there.

Three-Seeded Mercury *(Acalypha rhomboidea)*

OVERVIEW: This native annual is typically a foot high or less, but it can grow to 2 feet if left unchecked. It is generally unbranched; the **rounded** stem is **smooth or finely hairy**. Broken stems produce clear sap.

WHERE YOU'LL FIND IT: Gardens, alleys, fencelines, roadsides, streambanks, railroad tracks, ditches and disturbed areas. It prefers partial to full sun and can grow from pavement cracks. Three-Seeded Mercury is found in the eastern half of the U.S.; in our region it is largely absent from the Dakotas and the northern parts of Minnesota, Wisconsin and Michigan.

LEAVES: Elliptic, with tapered bases and sharply tapered tips; they often look somewhat **diamond-shaped**. Leaves are up to 4 inches long and a bit less than half as wide, and grow **alternately** on thin stalks that are up to **1½ inches long**. Edges are coarsely toothed. Leaves are sparsely hairy and green, turning **copper-colored** in fall.

FLOWERS/FRUIT: Tiny pale flowers grow in **small clusters at leaf axils**; they are **surrounded by small bracts, each with 5 to 9 lobes** (see small photo at right). Flowers are replaced by three-lobed capsules.

SEASON: Plants appear in late spring; flowers are present from mid-summer through fall.

OTHER NAMES: Rhomboid Mercury, Rhombic Copperleaf, Copperleaf.

COMPARE: Virginia Copperleaf (*A. virginica*) appears similar, but the bracts around the flowers have up to **15 lobes**, appearing **frilly**; stems are **fuzzy**. In our region, this native annual grows in the southern half. • Pennsylvania Pellitory (*Parietaria pensylvanica*) has narrow, **toothless** leaves with **short stalks** and somewhat **wavy** edges. The main stem is **square and hairy**. Flowers are surrounded by **multiple, unlobed bracts**. In our region, this native annual is found throughout except the northern parts of Minnesota, Wisconsin and Michigan. • Stinging Nettle (pg. 64) resembles young Three-Seeded Mercury, but Nettle leaves grow **oppositely** on **square** stems; flower clusters grow on **long stemlets**.

GETTING RID OF IT!

Three-Seeded Mercury has a shallow root system and is easy to pull when the soil has been softened by rain. Plants should be pulled before the flowers develop.

WHAT'S IT GOOD FOR?

Numerous bird species eat the seeds. Three-Seeded Mercury has reportedly been used medicinally, but is not considered edible (so be certain of your identification when looking for the similar-appearing Stinging Nettle for the table).

White Snakeroot

(Ageratina altissima)

OVERVIEW: Known as "the weed that killed Lincoln's mother," White Snakeroot is a native perennial that quickly becomes weedy-looking. It is from 1 to 4 feet tall and branches several times in the top portion. Its round stems are tan to light green, becoming stouter with maturity.

WHERE YOU'LL FIND IT: White Snakeroot thrives in moist to slightly dry areas with partial shade and rich soil. It is found in shady yards and gardens, as well as in abandoned lots that have some shade, thickets, powerline cuts, open deciduous woodlands and shelterbelts. It grows in the eastern half of the U.S., although not in the deep southeast; in our region it is absent from northern Minnesota, northern Michigan and most of the Dakotas.

LEAVES: Thin, egg-shaped leaves, 2 to 5 inches long with a broad base and narrow, pointed tip, grow oppositely on thin leafstalks that are about one-third the length of the leaf. Edges have **coarse teeth** all around except at the base. Each leaf has **3 main veins** that begin at the leaf stalk; side veins appear along the edges and from the top half of the central vein. Pale leaf miner trails are often visible in the leaves.

FLOWERS/FRUIT: Loose, branching flat-topped clusters of **fuzzy-looking** bright white flowers, each up to ½ inch across, grow at the ends of branching stems in the upper half of the plant. The clusters are 1 to 2 inches across. Flowers are replaced by black seeds, each with multiple fluffy white tufts of hair.

SEASON: White Snakeroot flowers from late summer to early fall; it is usually the only white wildflower in bloom in the forest at that time. It will bloom until the plants are killed by frost.

OTHER NAMES: Tall Boneset, *Eupatorium rugosum*.

COMPARE: Common Boneset (*E. perfoliatum*) has similar flat-topped clusters of white flowers, but its leaves are **joined at the base**; the **stem runs through the pair**. Its range is about the same as White Snakeroot.

GETTING RID OF IT!

White Snakeroot spreads by seed and also by rhizomes. It is fairly easy to pull if the soil is fresh and the stout stem is grasped near the base. Larger clumps should be dug out so you can get all the rhizomes.

WHAT'S IT GOOD FOR?

Although indigenous tribes reportedly used a decoction of the plant to treat snakebite, it appears to have little practical use other than to adorn the autumn woodlands. Milk from cows that eat the foliage causes milk sickness, a disease that plagued settlers and was considered the cause of the 1818 death of Nancy Lincoln, mother of future president Abraham Lincoln, in Indiana.

Japanese Knotweed

(Reynoutria japonica)

OVERVIEW: This perennial was brought to the U.S. from Asia for erosion control and as an ornamental. It has become a hard-to-control pest that is spreading widely and is often considered invasive. Stems are smooth and **reddish** or streaked with red; lower stems are stout and **hollow** and somewhat resemble bamboo. Plants may be up to 10 feet tall in favorable conditions. The leaf axils are **swollen** and the stem bends in a **zigzag** fashion between nodes. Plants branch frequently, and the tops are **very leafy**, creating a dense shade canopy. Stems die back to the ground in winter.

WHERE YOU'LL FIND IT: Prefers sunlight and rich, moist soil, but tolerates poor soil, shade and dry conditions. Colonies may develop on river banks that have been scoured by high water; it also grows on roadsides, in ditches and along the edges of ponds and streams. In our region, it is currently found in the eastern portion, with the heaviest infestations in Indiana, Michigan (including the Upper Peninsula), and the eastern parts of Illinois, Wisconsin and Ohio.

LEAVES: Egg-shaped leaves, with a **flat base** and a pointed tip, grow alternately on short stalks. They are up to 6 inches long and 4 inches wide.

FLOWERS/FRUIT: **Slender floral spikes**, up to 5 inches long, grow from leaf axils; each axil may have **two or more** spikes. The trumpet-shaped flowers are white and about ⅓ inch across; the leaflike sepals at the base turn reddish. Fruits are seeds with three broad, flat wings.

SEASON: Flowers are present from late summer into early fall.

OTHER NAMES: Japanese Bamboo, Japanese Fleece Flower, *Polygonum cuspidatum, Fallopia japonica.*

COMPARE: Giant Knotweed (*R. sachalinensis*) is similar, but leaves are up to **15 inches long** and have **heart-shaped bases**. It is rare in our area, but may spread here from the Eastern states, where it is taking hold.

GETTING RID OF IT!

Japanese Knotweed spreads by rhizomes, and can regenerate from a chunk that is an inch or less in size. Single plants can be pulled when young, but if left unchecked, the plants spread rapidly and create large colonies. Some sources report that frequent cutting, repeated for several years, will eventually clear a patch of Japanese Knotweed by exhausting the roots. Glyphosate is effective when sprayed several times each season, particularly in the fall before the plant dies back for winter.

WHAT'S IT GOOD FOR?

The roots are a source for resveratrol, an antioxidant compound that some claim will increase longevity and reduce heart problems.

Yellow Rocket

(Barbarea vulgaris)

OVERVIEW: This non-native biennial is typically 1 to 2 feet tall, with numerous branching stems in the upper half. Its multiple clusters of bright yellow flowers make it easy to spot from a distance. Up close, look for sturdy **ridged, hairless** stems that are greenish to reddish.

WHERE YOU'LL FIND IT: Found throughout our region, but rare to absent in the Dakotas. It is common in ditches, fencelines and hedgerows in rural and agricultural areas, and is increasingly being found on disturbed ground, in empty lots and along roadside embankments in urban areas.

LEAVES: Leaves are **smooth and rounded** with **wavy** edges. Basal leaves are up to 6 inches long, with up to **4 pairs of side lobes and a larger terminal lobe**; they grow on a long stemlet. Similar leaves ascend the stem alternately, becoming smaller and having fewer side lobes. The upper leaves are shallowly lobed, or wedge-shaped with rounded teeth; their bases clasp the stem.

FLOWERS/FRUIT: Racemes (pg. 17) of bright yellow flowers grow at stem ends. Individual flowers are ⅓ inch across; they have 4 petals and 6 stamens. The racemes elongate with maturity. Flowers develop into **slender, upward-curving seedpods** about 1 inch long that **grow sideways** from the stem. Lower flowers go to seed first; seedpod development progresses up the stem while the top is still flowering. With the curved seedpods, the plant resembles a thin-armed candelabra.

SEASON: Flowers appear from early to late spring; seedpods develop throughout summer.

OTHER NAMES: Winter Cress.

COMPARE: Many yellow-flowered members of the mustard family (Brassicaceae) appear similar at a quick glance. Some may appear in home gardens, but most are crop weeds. They are identified by leaf shape, flower size and the shape and arrangement of the fruits. Genera include *Barbarea, Brassica, Descurainia, Erysimum, Sinapis* and *Sisymbrium*.

Seedpods

GETTING RID OF IT!

Yellow Rocket is usually considered an invasive weed. It can be pulled when the soil is moist; this is best done before the seedpods develop, to avoid spreading the seeds. Mowing when the stem is present, but before flowering, will prevent the plant from flowering.

WHAT'S IT GOOD FOR?

Yellow Rocket is high in vitamins C and A. Young leaves may be eaten raw in small amounts, but are more often cooked like spinach; they are best combined with other greens to temper their strong flavor. The flowering heads resemble tiny broccoli, and can be steamed as a bitter vegetable. It was reportedly used medicinally by Native Cherokee peoples.

Common Groundsel
(Senecio vulgaris)

OVERVIEW: This non-native annual is easy to ignore; with its inconspicuous flowers, it just looks like another green weed. Closer inspection reveals a fairly interesting plant. It can grow to 18 inches in height, but is frequently shorter. Stems are smooth, hollow and fleshy; they are deep green, becoming purplish near the base. They branch frequently.

WHERE YOU'LL FIND IT: Disturbed areas with full or partial sun. It is common in urban areas, where it grows in parking lot borders, mulched areas, gardens, landscaped areas, along walls, next to sidewalks and along roads; it can grow from cracks in pavement. It is also found in fields and along railroad tracks. It is present throughout our region, but population maps are nonspecific as to population density in each state.

LEAVES: **Glossy**, somewhat **succulent** leaves grow alternately. Leaves at the base are up to 4 inches long, with wide stalks; they are **oblong** with numerous **rounded lobes**, resembling narrow oak leaves. Leaves become smaller as they ascend the stem, and lobes become deeper and more pointed; towards the top of the plant, leaves have no stalks and some leaves clasp the stem. Leaf edges tend to curl downward.

FLOWERS/FRUIT: Small clusters of flowers grow at stem ends. Flowerheads are ⅓ inch long and ¼ inch across, and consist of a **bullet-shaped green base** packed with tiny **yellow** disk florets that barely reach above the base. Seeds with tufts of white hairs replace the florets.

SEASON: In flower from spring through early summer. Plants shrivel in midsummer, then reappear and bloom again in late summer.

OTHER NAMES: Common Ragwort, Old-Man-in-the-Spring.

COMPARE: Pilewort (*Erechtites hieraciifolius*; also called Burnweed) has similar flowers, but the flowerheads are about **¾ inch** long with **white** florets. Leaves are broadly **lance-shaped** and up to **8 inches** long; they have **jagged teeth** around the edges. Plants are 2 to **8 feet** tall. In our region, it is found in the eastern two-thirds.

Common Groundsel

Pilewort

GETTING RID OF IT!

Common Groundsel reproduces by seed and will be killed by frost. It has a shallow taproot and is easy to pull; hoeing is also effective. Because it produces prolific amounts of seeds, it must be dealt with before the seeds develop and float away in the breeze to start new plants. Mulch will prevent wind-blown seeds from other locations from sprouting in your garden. It is resistant to some herbicides.

WHAT'S IT GOOD FOR?

It is said that Common Groundsel is one of the most common weeds in the world. It has been used as a fresh, leafy food for poultry and cage birds; however, it can cause liver poisoning in horses, cattle and swine.

Little-Leaf Buttercup

(Ranunculus abortivus)

OVERVIEW: This common native annual can be up to 20 inches tall, but it is usually 10 inches or less. Its smooth, branching stems are long and slender, making the plant appear somewhat delicate.

WHERE YOU'LL FIND IT: Found throughout our region, although it is less common in the Dakotas. Little-Leaf Buttercup prefers moist areas with dappled sunlight. In urban parks that are mowed, it may thrive in spots the mower can't reach, such as at the base of trees. It also grows along garden edges and fences.

LEAVES: Two types of leaves are present. A cluster of **kidney-shaped leaves with scalloped edges** grows on long, thin stalks at the base of the plant; some may be lobed. Basal leaves are up to 2½ inches wide and 2 inches deep. Leaves on the stem are **elliptic or lobed** and up to 1½ inches long; those on the lower stems grow alternately on long stalks, while the upper leaves are sessile and may appear whorled.

FLOWERS/FRUIT: Tiny flowers, **¼ inch across**, grow on thin stemlets from branch tips. The **dome-like** center is bright green and surrounded by 5 **triangular** yellow petals; 5 **rounded green sepals** sit below the petals.

SEASON: Flowers appear from mid-spring to early summer.

OTHER NAMES: Small-Flowered Buttercup, Early Wood Buttercup, Kidney-Leaf Buttercup.

COMPARE: Cursed Crowfoot (*R. sceleratus*; also called Cursed Buttercup) appears similar, but the basal leaves always have 3 to 5 lobes which may be shallow or deep; most stem leaves have **3 deeply cleft lobes**, although a few leaves at the top of the stem may be unlobed and sessile. The leaves are somewhat **thick and fleshy**. Flowers are slightly larger than those of Little-Leaf Buttercup and have **rounded** petals. Cursed Crowfoot is scattered throughout our region, and is found in wetter habitat than Little-Leaf Buttercup. It is an annual or a short-lived perennial.

GETTING RID OF IT!

Hand-pulling works well when the soil is moist; wear gloves to prevent contact dermatitis. Mowing will control light populations.

WHAT'S IT GOOD FOR?

Little-Leaf Buttercup is pleasant to look at, but like all Buttercups it may cause skin irritation when handled. It is toxic to both humans and livestock when eaten fresh. When broken, the stem and leaves of Cursed Crowfoot ooze sap that may cause blisters, accounting for the "cursed" designation.

Wild Parsnip

(Pastinaca sativa)

OVERVIEW: Wild Parsnip can be a dangerous plant to the unaware. This non-native biennial contains chemicals called furocoumarins that can cause a condition called *phytophotodermatitis*. The reaction occurs when moist skin comes in contact with the juice from broken stems or bruised leaves and is then exposed to sunlight. Several hours to 3 days later, serious blistering can occur, although the reaction may be less severe or absent (and rare when contact is made with first-year rosettes; the second-year plant is the culprit here). The blisters can leave behind dark scars that take a long time—sometimes years—to heal. First-year plants are a basal rosette. Second-year plants have a **ridged** stem that is 3 to 6 feet tall; the plants branch occasionally near the top.

WHERE YOU'LL FIND IT: Wild Parsnip is typically an agricultural weed that is found in sunny, moist spots such as fields and pastures, but it also grows along roads—even major highways. It is found primarily in the eastern two-thirds of our region and is listed as a noxious weed in Ohio.

LEAVES: Compound leaves with **4 or 5 paired leaflets** (typically) plus a terminal leaflet grow in a basal rosette, and also alternately along the stems of second-year plants. Leaflets are elliptic and hairless, with **coarse teeth**; they may also have one or more lobes. Basal leaves are up to **18 inches long** and one-third as wide, and grow on a long stalk; stem leaves are smaller, with fewer leaflets and short stalks.

FLOWERS/FRUIT: **Flat-topped floral clusters**, 3 to 8 inches across, grow on leafless stalks from the ends of branching stems. The large cluster is made up of smaller clusters of ⅛-inch yellow flowers. Fruit is a flat, oval green seedpod that turns brown and splits to release a single seed.

SEASON: Flowers are present from late spring to midsummer.

OTHER NAMES: Common Parsnip, *Panais Sauvage*.

COMPARE: Cow Parsnip (pg. 78) has similar robust leaves and a large, flat flowering cluster, but its flowers are **white**.

First-year basal rosette

GETTING RID OF IT!

Wild Parsnip has a long tap root. Second-year plants can be pulled from moist soil, assisted by a flat-toothed garden fork if necessary; roots can also be cut off an inch below the soil with a sharp shovel, and the plants pulled after that. Wear gloves, long sleeves and pants when working around Wild Parsnip. Basal clusters will be killed by triclopyr or glyphosate, but you may choose to harvest the roots for the table; see below.

WHAT'S IT GOOD FOR?

According to foraging expert Sam Thayer, Wild Parsnip is the same plant as domesticated parsnip. Roots of the first-year plants are edible, and can be prepared with any recipe used for domestic parsnips.

Yellow Sweet-Clover

(Melilotus officinalis)

OVERVIEW: Here's another plant that was brought from Eurasia to the U.S. as a livestock forage crop, but which has become pervasive, and invasive, throughout most of the country. It is a leafy annual or biennial up to 6 feet tall; larger plants branch frequently and often appear somewhat **airy** in the upper parts. Stems are **ridged** and greenish, sometimes with a reddish tint in the lower parts. It often grows in colonies.

WHERE YOU'LL FIND IT: This plant is very common in urban areas, where it is seen in vacant lots, along roadsides and railroad tracks, and in weedy edges surrounding parks and athletic fields; it also grows in open fields, weedy meadows and prairies. It is common throughout our region.

LEAVES: Three-part compound leaves grow alternately on **thin stalks** up to 1 inch long; 2 small leaflike stipules generally grow at the base. Leaflets are elliptic to oblong and **bluish-green**; they are ½ to 1 inch long and half as wide. Edges have **fine teeth**.

FLOWERS/FRUIT: Racemes (pg. 17) of bright **yellow pea-like** flowers with 5 petals grow at the tops of the main and branching stems and also on stems arising from leaf axils. Flowers are about ⅓ inch long and **droop downward**. They are replaced by oval seedpods, less than ⅛ inch long, that are initially green, ripening to dark brown or blackish.

SEASON: Flowers are present from late spring through late summer.

OTHER NAMES: Yellow Melilot, Common Melilot.

COMPARE: A **white-flowered** version of this plant is usually called White Sweet-Clover. Some sources consider the white-flowered version to be simply a variation of the yellow-flowered plants, and use the name *M. officinalis alba*. Other sources treat *M. alba* as a distinct species and note that the white-flowered version is slightly taller (up to 8 feet) and blooms a bit later than the yellow-flowered one. It apparently grows in the same areas as the yellow-flowered version.

GETTING RID OF IT!

Hand pulling can be used on small populations as long as the plants are pulled before the seedpods appear; pull when the soil is moist so the long taproot can be removed, or cut the root off a few inches below the soil before pulling. Mowing provides mixed results with large populations; it is most effective when used early in the flowering period because it will cause the plants to expend energy to regrow the stems, thus weakening the roots. Additional mowing may be needed when the plants regrow.

WHAT'S IT GOOD FOR?

Honeybees flock to blooming patches of both Yellow and White Sweet Clover; other types of bees and insects also visit the plants to gather pollen and nectar. Plants are eaten by rabbits, deer and other animals.

Leafy Spurge

(Euphorbia esula)

OVERVIEW: With its **greenish to yellow flowers nestled in little cups**, and smooth stem with long, narrow leaves, this non-native perennial is easy to recognize. It is usually **1 to 3 feet** tall; several floral stems often branch out at the top. All parts ooze **milky sap** when crushed or broken.

WHERE YOU'LL FIND IT: Disturbed locations with plenty of sun, including landscaped areas, prairies, dry fields, railroad embankments, waste ground, roadsides and scrubby edges of urban parks; this is not an agricultural weed. In our region, Leafy Spurge is found throughout the northwestern two-thirds, and it is listed as a noxious weed in South Dakota, North Dakota, Minnesota, Iowa and Wisconsin.

LEAVES: Smooth, **linear** leaves, up to 3 inches long with a prominent mid-vein, grow alternately, attached directly to the stem (sessile) and **widely spaced** on the stem. Leaf edges are smooth; the tip is softly pointed.

FLOWERS/FRUIT: Spurges have an unusual-looking floral arrangement called a cyathium (plural: cyathia). A pair of oval bracts form a **cup** about ⅓ inch across. In the center, a single, ornate female flower is flanked by 2 (typically) rounded male flowers. Bracts and flowers are **yellowish-green**. The cyathia grow from leaf axils on long, thin stemlets, and also in clusters at the tops of the branching and main stems; a whorl of small leaves grows under the clusters. The fruit is a long, 3-valved capsule that dispenses seeds explosively, up to 15 feet away.

SEASON: The cyathia begin developing in spring, and the plants flower from late spring through early fall

OTHER NAMES: Wolf's Milk, *E. virgata*.

COMPARE: Cypress Spurge (*E. cyparissias*; non-native perennial) looks rather like a miniature version of Leafy Spurge. It is a foot high or less, with very narrow leaves that grow **fairly closely together** on the stem. It blooms a month earlier than Leafy Spurge. In our region, it is fairly well distributed in all states except the Dakotas, where it may be absent.

GETTING RID OF IT!

Leafy Spurge is highly invasive. It has a deep, expansive root system, and root fragments can produce new plants. Hand pulling must be followed with digging to remove as much of the roots as possible. Goats can eat the plants with no ill effects, and experiments involving the use of browsing goats to control Leafy Spurge have been encouraging.

WHAT'S IT GOOD FOR?

Mourning doves eat the seeds, and the plants are important for nesting western meadowlarks. However, the plants produce chemicals that inhibit growth of other plants. Cattle and horses that eat it become sick, and some studies suggest that it may be carcinogenic to humans.

Yellow Wood Sorrel

(Oxalis stricta)

OVERVIEW: This weedy native perennial often appears as a low-growing plant, but it may be up to a foot tall in areas that don't get mowed. Stems are **thin and greenish**, sometimes with a reddish cast; they are typically fuzzy but may be hairless. Plants may branch frequently towards the base, and each root may produce several stems.

WHERE YOU'LL FIND IT: Full sun to partial shade, in dry to slightly moist areas including lawns, gardens, landscape plantings, roadsides, alleys, rocky or gravelly areas, waste areas, open woods, meadows—in short, just about everywhere. It is quite common throughout our area, although it is less reported in the Dakotas.

LEAVES: Three-part compound leaves with **reversed heart-shaped** leaflets (with the point towards the leaf stalk) grow alternately on long, thin stalks. Edges are untoothed; the lower surface is slightly hairy. Leaflets are ¼ to ½ inch across; they may **fold together** along the central veins in the evening and on cool or cloudy days.

FLOWERS/FRUIT: Bright yellow flowers, about ¼ inch across, have **5 petals** with rounded tips and tapered bases. They grow in small clusters on long stemlets originating from leaf axils in the upper part of the plant. The fruits that replace them are oblong green capsules.

SEASON: Wood Sorrel blooms from late spring through early fall.

OTHER NAMES: Lemon Clover, Sourgrass, Woodsorrel.

COMPARE: Clovers have 3-part compound leaves, but leaflets are **rounded or oval** rather than heart-shaped. The Clovers on pg. 32 have **white, reddish, pinkish or purplish** flowers. The flowerheads are **globe-shaped** and typically ¾ to 1 inch across, with numerous thin individual flowers clustered together. • Black Medick, Golden Clover and Hop Clover (pg. 42) have 3-part leaves and yellow flowers, but the leaflets are **oval**. Flowerheads are **globe-shaped** and ¼ to ½ inch across.

**Folded leaves
(right)**

GETTING RID OF IT!

Hand pulling can be effective for young plants; be sure to get the roots to prevent regrowth, and continue to pull new plants as they appear. Prevention is the best strategy; encouraging healthy growth of other plants prevents Wood Sorrel seeds from germinating. Mulching is also effective at discouraging Wood Sorrel growth. If herbicides are used, they should be applied on a sunny day, when the leaves are fully open.

WHAT'S IT GOOD FOR?

Leaves, flowers and green seed capsules are all edible, with a lemony-sour flavor. You may enjoy munching on them as you are weeding.

Curly Dock

(Rumex crispus)

OVERVIEW: This non-native perennial is easy to identify. In early spring, it is a **basal rosette** of **oblong, deep green leaves** with **wavy edges**. By late spring, it produces a **stout, ribbed** round stem that grows rapidly and can be up to 5 feet tall at maturity, although it is usually shorter. Flowers develop on branching clusters at the top of the plant.

WHERE YOU'LL FIND IT: Dry to moist areas with full to part sun. In urban areas, Curly Dock is a very common sight along highways and city streets, in vacant lots and scrubby park edges, along railroad tracks and in alleys; it also grows in old fields and in weedy pastures. It is common throughout our region and, indeed, throughout most of the U.S.

LEAVES: The oblong to nearly lance-like leaves are hairless and **curled**, with a pale central rib and **ruffled or crinkly edges**. Leaves in the basal cluster are up to 12 inches long and one-third as wide; they grow on long, stout stalks (petioles). Stem leaves are shorter and have shorter petioles. A **papery sheath** (called an ocrea) wraps around the stem at each leaf node, but it deteriorates quickly.

FLOWERS/FRUIT: Yellowish to red-tinged flowers, about $\frac{1}{8}$ inch across, grow in clusters on stalks at the top of the plant. Flowers have several leaflike sepals but no petals; each plant contains both female flowers and perfect (bisexual) flowers that droop down on short stemlets. Each flower produces a single seed that is encased in a flat, brown wing-like structure. The **tall flower stalks with brown seed masses** are a common sight in late summer.

SEASON: Flowers are present from early summer to midsummer; the brown seed masses persist into fall.

OTHER NAMES: Curled Dock, Yellow Dock.

COMPARE: Pale Dock (*R. altissimus*; native perennial) is shorter than Curly Dock, and its leaves are **flat**. It has **no basal rosette**, and is 4 feet or less in height. In our region, it is concentrated in Iowa and Illinois.

Young plant

Flowers

GETTING RID OF IT!

Curly Dock has a large, forked taproot that is difficult to pull without breaking it off, and any portions that are left in the ground will produce new plants. Use a flat-tined garden fork to gently work around the root, loosening the soil to a depth of at least a foot; this should be done when the soil is moist. Slide a sturdy, broad-bladed knife along the root and gently tease it out. Dock plants produce hundreds of seeds, so removal needs to take place before the plants flower.

WHAT'S IT GOOD FOR?

Leaves are edible when steamed or boiled; they have a somewhat sour flavor and become dull, army green. The roots are used medicinally.

St. John's Wort

(Hypericum perforatum)

OVERVIEW: Although it has very showy flowers, this non-native perennial spreads aggressively and forms large colonies; it is highly invasive in some areas. Common St. John's Wort is up to 18 inches tall. The stems are smooth and **branch very frequently**; the side branches are very leafy and grow oppositely at an **upward angle**.

WHERE YOU'LL FIND IT: Areas with full sun, with medium to low soil moisture. It is frequently seen along roads and railroads, in pastures and in open woodlands. In urban areas it is becoming increasingly common in vacant lots, poorly tended landscaped areas and scrubby parks. In our region it is found primarily in the eastern two-thirds, including eastern Minnesota and Iowa. It is listed as a noxious weed in South Dakota.

LEAVES: Oblong to elliptic leaves about 1 inch long grow oppositely, attached directly to the stems (sessile). The leaves are hairless, and scattered with numerous **dot-like oil sacs** that are **translucent** when the leaf is held up to the light (see small photo at right). Leaf undersides often have a few **black dots** scattered around the edges.

FLOWERS/FRUIT: Flat-topped clusters of flowers (cymes) grow at the ends of the upper stems. Flowers are about 1 inch across, with 5 oval yellow petals. Petals have **fine black dots scattered around the edges**; these are more oil sacs that **stain fingers red** if the petals are rubbed. The center of the flower is crowded with yellow-tipped stamens. The fruit is a pointed capsule that turns deep reddish-brown with maturity.

SEASON: Flowers are present from early summer to midsummer.

OTHER NAMES: Common St. John's Wort, St. Johnswort, Klamath Weed.

COMPARE: Spotted St. John's Wort (*H. punctatum*; native) is similar, but its leaves have **numerous black dots overall** and **lack the translucent dots**. Flower petals have fine black dots and streaks **overall**. Its range in our area is a bit more easterly than that of Common St. John's Wort; it is not found in the Dakotas, most of Minnesota or northwestern Iowa.

A large infestation (above); oil sacs on leaves (right)

GETTING RID OF IT!

Common St. John's Wort has a deep, branched taproot and spreading rhizomes. Young plants and small patches can be dug out, taking care to get all of the root system. Larger infestations require serious digging or the use of herbicides; 2, 4-D is apparently one of the better choices.

WHAT'S IT GOOD FOR?

Common St. John's Wort is a well-known and much-used herbal remedy for depression and sleeplessness; the medication is made from the oil sacs on both the leaves and flowers. St. John's Wort tea is also used medicinally. A red dye can be obtained from the oil sacs on the flowers. The foliage is poisonous to livestock.

Birdsfoot Trefoil

(Lotus corniculatus)

OVERVIEW: Originally imported from Europe for livestock forage, this little plant, with its profusion of charming yellow flowers, has overstayed its welcome and has a bad habit of overrunning native vegetation. Birdsfoot Trefoil is classified as invasive in Illinois, Wisconsin and Minnesota, as well as other states outside our region. Its thin stems can be 2 feet long, but it often sprawls on the ground. It is a perennial that spreads rapidly and forms dense colonies.

WHERE YOU'LL FIND IT: Sunny areas such as roadsides, boulevards, parks, landscape plantings and prairies. In our region, it is concentrated in Minnesota, Wisconsin, Indiana and the northern two-thirds of Illinois.

LEAVES: Five-part compound leaves grow alternately on short stalks. The 3 leaflets at the top of the stalk are teardrop-shaped with tapered bases that are joined together; **2 additional leaflets with broad bases grow a short distance away** at the base of the leaf stalk. Leaflets are ½ to ¾ inch long with smooth edges; tips are pointed or rounded.

FLOWERS/FRUIT: Bright yellow **pea-like** flowers have **one large, rounded central petal facing upwards, with smaller petals at the base that are folded over the pistil and stamen**. The large central petal often has darker streaks radiating from its center. Flowers in full sunlight may turn orangish with red streaks. The flowers grow in a **whorl of 3 to 8** at the top of a long, thin leafless stalk that originates in a leaf axil. Flowers are replaced by slender seedpods up to 1 inch long; the cluster of seedpods resembles a bird's foot, accounting for the common name.

SEASON: Birdsfoot Trefoil is in flower from early through late summer.

OTHER NAMES: Birdfoot Deervetch, Yellow Trefoil, Devil's Claw.

COMPARE: Yellow Toadflax (pg. 128) also has a profusion of bright yellow flowers, but they have a **long spur** at the bottom and their leaves are **linear**.

GETTING RID OF IT!

Birdsfoot Trefoil reproduces by seed and has a branching taproot. Mowing will help control it, but frequent pulling is more effective in eradicating this pest. The presence of Birdsfoot Trefoil may signal low levels of nitrogen; soil amendments, including compost and compost tea, may help prevent its regrowth. Prescribed burns in prairie areas encourage Birdsfoot Trefoil seed germination, increasing the threat this plant poses to native prairie species.

WHAT'S IT GOOD FOR?

It works well for erosion control, and even though it is classified as invasive in numerous states it is still sold in seed mixtures.

Yellow Toadflax

(Linaria vulgaris)

OVERVIEW: This Eurasian native, with its charming yellow-and-gold flowers, was introduced as a garden ornamental, and has become an invasive plant that develops large colonies. It has an **unbranched** central stem that is typically about a foot high, but can become taller.

WHERE YOU'LL FIND IT: Typically found in dry, sunny areas with bare soil. In urban areas it grows in boulevards, parking-lot islands, scrubby areas of parks, ill-kept gardens and along roads and railroad tracks. It is also found in pastures and open fields; it is quite a pest in prairies because fire does not reduce its population, allowing it to outcompete native prairie species. This perennial is found throughout our region, and is on the noxious weeds list in South Dakota.

LEAVES: Linear, smooth-edges leaves up to 3 inches long and 3/16 inch wide are attached directly to the stem (sessile). They grow alternately, but are usually so **closely spaced** that they appear opposite or whorled. All leaves on a plant are about the **same length**.

FLOWERS/FRUIT: Yellow **snapdragon-like** flowers, 3/4 to 1 inch long, grow closely together on a long floral spike at the top of the plant. Between the upper and lower yellow petals is a **deep gold to orangish tongue-like throat**; a long, pointed **yellow nectar spur** hangs at the bottom of each flower. The fruits are oval capsules that contain many seeds.

SEASON: Flowers are present from early to late summer.

OTHER NAMES: Butter-and-Eggs, Wild Snapdragon.

COMPARE: Dalmatian Toadflax (*L. dalmatica*) has similar flowers, but the throat generally lacks the deep color. More significantly, the leaves are **oval, waxy and bluish-green**, with a **broad base** up to 1½ inches wide and a narrow, pointed tip; they resemble **tulip leaves**. Leaf bases clasp the stems. Dalmatian Toadflax is most common in the western U.S. but is gradually creeping into our area; it is on the noxious weeds list in the Dakotas, where it is found in numerous counties.

GETTING RID OF IT!

Both of the Toadflax listed here have deep, spreading roots that send up new shoots; they also reproduce by seed. Some populations have become resistant to herbicides. Frequent mowing will control the above-ground portions and can be used to prevent flowers from producing seed, but mowing will not control the underground root system. Hand pulling will not eliminate the roots, but will gradually weaken the plants. The best strategy is frequent pulling, followed by long-term mulching.

WHAT'S IT GOOD FOR?

Flowers attract bees, butterflies and other insects. Toadflax can be used to produce a yellow dye.

Tall Buttercup
(Ranunculus acris)

OVERVIEW: Unlike most Buttercups that grow in our region, Tall Buttercup is non-native, imported from Eurasia as an ornamental. This perennial is a rather **spindly-looking** plant, with leaves mostly at the bottom and thin stems that branch occasionally. Plants are up to **3 feet** high.

WHERE YOU'LL FIND IT: This plant prefers sunny locations with adequate moisture, and has become naturalized in areas such as moist fields, county roadsides, damp hay meadows, grasslands, gravel pits, woodland edges and streambanks. It also appears in gardens, lawns, parks and landscape plantings. It is most concentrated in northern states; in our region, it is found primarily in the northern half, creeping down around the Great Lakes into northern Illinois and northeast Ohio.

LEAVES: Three- to 5-lobed leaves with an overall **pentagonal** shape are key to identifying this species. These lobes are **deeply cleft**; lobe bases meet in a small area at the end of a long leaf stalk. Each of the lobes has additional lobed divisions with pointed tips. Leaves at the base of the plant are abundant and up to 5 inches across. A few smaller leaves grow on the branching stems; these leaves have narrower segments and look somewhat **spidery**. Leaf surfaces have soft, fine hairs.

FLOWERS/FRUIT: Deep yellow flowers grow singly or in small clusters atop long floral stalks that arise from leaf axils. Flowers are about 1 inch across and have 5 rounded, **glossy** petals that **overlap** slightly; a ring of yellow stamens surrounds the pale greenish pistils. Each flower is replaced by a rounded ¼-inch-wide cluster of smooth, oval green seeds.

SEASON: Tall Buttercup blooms from early to late summer.

OTHER NAMES: Meadow Buttercup, Common Buttercup, Giant Buttercup.

COMPARE: Bristly Buttercup (*R. hispidus*; native) is a woodland flower about a foot tall that is not weedy. **Three-part compound leaves** grow on long stalks; leaflets are 3-lobed and up to 4 inches long. Flower petals **do not overlap**. Found throughout our area, rare in the Dakotas.

Tall Buttercup   Bristly Buttercup

GETTING RID OF IT!

Tall Buttercup spreads by seed and also vegetatively, by rhizomes that divide to form new plant clusters. The main root is short, and pulling young plants in spring or early summer, before the rhizomes divide, is most effective. Cut older plants down before the seedpods develop.

WHAT'S IT GOOD FOR?

Portions of the plant have been used medicinally as poultices. Although some sources say that leaves are edible, ingestion is highly discouraged; Tall Buttercup contains toxins that cause blisters on the mouth and lips of livestock, as well as intestinal illnesses (and is probably none too good for humans, either).

Rough Cinquefoil

(Potentilla norvegica)

OVERVIEW: Rough Cinquefoil can be an annual, a biennial or a short-lived perennial. Many sources consider it to be non-native, but others list it as native. It starts as a basal rosette that develops a central stem up to 3 feet tall; multiple stems can grow from the base. The upper half also branches repeatedly, so plants become quite **bushy-looking**. Stems are **hairy** and greenish, often becoming reddish.

WHERE YOU'LL FIND IT: Often found in disturbed areas with other weedy plants. It grows in sunny areas as well as those with moderate shade, and is found along alleys and roads, weedy park edges, and in scrubby parking-lot borders and waste ground; also grows in meadows, old pastures and along creeks. It is fairly common throughout our region.

LEAVES: The **3-part compound leaves** are oblong with large, rounded teeth around the edges; they look like **narrow strawberry leaves**. Leaf stalks of the basal cluster are up to 6 inches long; the leaflets on these basal clusters are up to 2 inches long. Stem leaves are smaller and have short stalks; they become stalkless towards the top of the stems. All leaves are **medium-green on both sides** and moderately hairy.

FLOWERS/FRUIT: Bright yellow, 5-petaled flowers are up to ½ inch across, with a **dome-shaped** center; flowers grow singly or in small groups at stem ends. Petals are **rounded** to somewhat heart-shaped; the pointed green sepals at the base are **longer than the petals**. The sepals fold inward to protect the seeds that develop in the center.

SEASON: Rough Cinquefoil blooms from early to late summer.

OTHER NAMES: Norwegian Cinquefoil, Strawberry Weed.

COMPARE: Sulfur Cinquefoil (*P. recta*) has **narrower** leaflets with **pale** undersides. Lower leaves have **5 to 9** leaflets up to **3 inches** long; upper leaves have 3 to 5 leaflets. Flowers have **pale yellow** petals that are **longer than the sepals**. This non-native perennial is found throughout our region except the western third, where it is uncommon or absent.

Rough Cinquefoil   Sulfur Cinquefoil

GETTING RID OF IT!

These Cinquefoils reproduce by seed, so the key to long-term control is to prevent the flowers from producing seed. Young plants can be pulled out when the soil is loose; for more mature plants, dig out as much of the root crown as possible to prevent resprouting. Sulfur Cinquefoil also spreads with rhizomes that separate to create new plant clusters; it is considered a noxious weed in parts of the western U.S.

WHAT'S IT GOOD FOR?

Cinquefoil roots and leaves have astringent properties; poultices and decoctions have been used medicinally to treat sore throats and open wounds. The flowers are a food source for bees and other insects.

Common Mullein *(Verbascum thapsus)*

OVERVIEW: Mullein is a non-native biennial, flowering in its second year. The first-year plant is a rosette of leaves. Second-year plants grow rapidly and can be up to 6 feet tall; they are very leafy before and during flowering, and typically unbranched.

WHERE YOU'LL FIND IT: Areas in full sun, in dry to moderately dry soil. It is quite common in both rural and urban areas, and prefers disturbed spots such as vacant lots and other waste ground, weedy ground next to buildings, and along alleys, roadsides, freeway embankments and railroad tracks. It also grows in fields, prairies and limestone glades. Common Mullein is found in all states of our region, although it is uncommon in North Dakota and the northern half of South Dakota.

LEAVES: Oblong leaves with rounded or softly pointed tips are large and **densely fuzzy** at all stages of growth, with a **felt-like** texture. The first-year basal rosette is up to 2 feet across. Leaves of second-year plants grow alternately; those at the base are often **12 to 15 inches long** and 4 to 5 inches across, attached to the stalk with **winged bases**. As the leaves ascend the stem, they become smaller and no longer have the wings; the leaf bases tend to lie flat against the stem.

FLOWERS/FRUIT: The flowers grow densely together on a **thick floral spike** at the top of the stem. Unopened flowers are dull green and hairy. Only a handful of flowers are open at any given time; they are yellow and about ¾ inch across, with 5 fuzzy petals. The spike elongates and becomes thinner over the season, and is eventually covered in seed-bearing **brown, oval capsules** that replace the flowers.

SEASON: Mullein blooms from early summer through early fall. Empty seed capsules remain on the now-leafless floral spike through winter.

OTHER NAMES: Great Mullein, Velvet Plant, Flannel Plant and many other names that reflect the fuzzy nature of the leaves.

COMPARE: Nothing else in our region resembles Common Mullein.

GETTING RID OF IT!

Pulling is effective for small plants; larger second-year plants that are too big to pull should be cut off a few inches below the soil line. Second-year plants can be mowed prior to flowering, which will prevent the plants from releasing seeds. Mowing is not effective for first-year rosettes, as they will simply regrow; digging them out is a better solution.

WHAT'S IT GOOD FOR?

Tea made from Mullein leaves or flowers (strained before drinking to remove the fine hairs) has been used to treat respiratory problems. Native peoples used Mullein leaf poultices to treat bruises and other conditions. Bumblebees gather both nectar and pollen from Mullein flowers.

Sowthistle

(Sonchus spp.)

OVERVIEW: Sowthistle flowers resemble Dandelions (pg. 36), but Sowthistle plants are up to 4 feet tall, with leaves along the stem rather than just the simple basal cluster of the Dandelion. The Sowthistles listed here are non-native and found in all states of our region.

WHERE YOU'LL FIND IT: Disturbed places, ball fields, roadsides and alleys.

LEAVES: Sowthistles start as a basal cluster; stem leaves grow alternately. • Leaves of Perennial Sowthistle (*S. arvensis*; perennial) have **soft prickles** around the edges; the pale rib underneath has **no prickles**. Leaves on the lower stem are closely spaced; they are up to **12 inches** long and generally have several rounded lobes with pointed tips. At the base of the leaf, two **rounded lobes** clasp the stem. Leaves at the top of the stem are smaller and more widely spaced, and may be unlobed. • Lobes on the leaves of Common Sowthistle (*S. oleraceus*; annual) are **angular**; lower leaves have stalks and are up to 8 inches long. Upper leaves have lobes that clasp the stem; the **lobe tips are sharply pointed and extend past the stem**, encircling it. • Leaves of Spiny Sowthistle (*S. asper*; annual) are **shiny** and up to 10 inches long; they may be lobed or without lobes, but will have **long, prickly teeth** along the edges. Leaf bases have **rounded, prickly lobes** that clasp the stem.

FLOWERS/FRUIT: Flowers of the Sowthistles listed here strongly resemble Dandelions. Perennial Sowthistle has flowers up to **2 inches across**; flowers of Common and Spiny Sowthistle are less than an inch across. Like Dandelions, the flower turns into seeds with fluffy white hairs.

SEASON: Sowthistles are in flower from summer through fall.

OTHER NAMES: Some sources list *S. oleraceus* as Annual Sowthistle. Spiny Sowthistle is also called Prickly Sowthistle.

COMPARE: Leaves of Prickly Lettuce (pg. 138), which also has Dandelion-like flowers, resemble those of Perennial Sowthistle, but they have spines **on the midrib underneath** as well as around the leaf edges.

Common Sowthistle

Perennial Sowthistle

Spiny Sowthistle

GETTING RID OF IT!

Perennial Sowthistle reproduces both by seed and by its root system, which is very deep. Even small root fragments can produce new plants, so it can take several years of diligence to eliminate it. With all Sow-thistles, weeding or mowing is most effective before the plants flower.

WHAT'S IT GOOD FOR?

Leaves of young Perennial and Common Sowthistles are a good edible; older leaves tend to be bitter. It's best to trim off the spines from Spiny Sowthistle, which makes them a nuisance to prepare. Some people roast Sowthistle roots, then grind them to use as a coffee substitute. Sow-thistles are also used medicinally. The flowers provide food for bees.

Prickly Lettuce

(Lactuca serriola)

OVERVIEW: This native plant is typically an annual, but may grow as a biennial. It has a smooth, round green or whitish stem that is unbranched except for the floral stems that branch at the top. Prickly lettuce can grow to monstrous sizes if left unchecked; the author has seen plants well over head height, and some sources say it can reach 10 feet. Stems and leaves ooze **milky sap** when crushed or broken.

WHERE YOU'LL FIND IT: Sun to part shade; it can grow in poor soil. It is found in gardens, boulevards, and along roadsides and railroad tracks; it also flourishes in disturbed areas such as vacant lots, dumps and waste ground. In our region, it is common except in the far north.

LEAVES: Although they are variable in shape, all leaves share one defining characteristic: The midvein on the underside is pale and has **short, pale prickles along the entire length**. Leaves can be oblong with shallow or deep lobes that may appear tooth-like; they can also be lance-like. Edges are toothy and have **tiny spines**. Leaves near the base are up to a foot long; they become smaller and less lobed towards the top of the plant. They grow alternately, attached directly to the stem (sessile); two lobes at the base of each leaf **clasp the stem**.

FLOWERS/FRUIT: Yellow dandelion-like flowers are ¼ to ½ inch across, and grow in large, open clusters on long stemlets at the top of the stem; floral stems also grow from leaf axils at the upper part of the plant. Like Dandelions, the flowers are replaced with fluffy white seedheads.

SEASON: Flowers are present from midsummer through early fall.

OTHER NAMES: Opium Lettuce, *L. scariola*.

COMPARE: Wild Lettuce (*L. canadensis*; also called Canada Lettuce) is a native biennial that also has leaves of variable shape, but they **lack the prickles** on the midvein. Stems are green or purplish, typically with **purple spots, blotches or streaks**. In our area, it is found in all states except the Dakotas; its range extends to the Canadian border.

GETTING RID OF IT!

The tall, leafy stems of both Lettuces described here are easy to remove by pulling, even when plants have gotten quite large (and your yard will look *so* much better without them), but you won't get the deep taproot unless you dig for it. Lettuces reproduce by seed, so you should remove the stems before the seedheads develop. Sheep and goats can be used for control in rural areas, although the taproots will continue to produce new growth for the rest of the season.

WHAT'S IT GOOD FOR?

The sap is reportedly used medicinally. Some people eat the young leaves, which have a bitter flavor and are said to be good for digestion.

Tansy

(Tanacetum vulgare)

OVERVIEW: This non-native perennial was brought to the U.S. from Eurasia as an ornamental and medicinal plant, and it has become a highly invasive weed. It is typically 2 to 4 feet tall and branches occasionally. Stems are smooth or slightly hairy; they are often reddish or purplish, particularly towards the bottom of the plant.

WHERE YOU'LL FIND IT: Full sun to light shade. It tolerates a variety of soil types and moisture. In natural areas it is found in prairies, meadows and woodland edges, as well as in rocky areas along lakeshores. It is also a notorious roadside weed in both rural and more populated areas. In our region, it is found primarily in the northern half; it is particularly common in Wisconsin, Michigan's Upper Peninsula, and the northern parts of Minnesota and Illinois.

LEAVES: Compound, **fern-like** leaves with 4 to 10 pairs of **flat** leaflets grow alternately. Leaves are up to 8 inches long and about half as wide at the base; leaflets are oblong, with toothy edges. The leaves have a **strong, camphor-like odor**.

FLOWERS/FRUIT: Bright yellow flowerheads about ¼ inch across grow in profusion in **flat clusters** at the top of the plant, and on long stalks growing from leaf axils. Flowerheads are made of tiny disk florets that are bunched together in a **flat, button-like disk**; there are **no ray florets** (petals). Dark brown seedheads replace the flowers in fall.

SEASON: Flowers are present from midsummer through early fall.

OTHER NAMES: Golden Buttons, Bitter Buttons, *Chrysanthemum vulgare*.

COMPARE: Its leaves somewhat resemble those of Dog Fennel (pg. 90), another malodorous plant, but Dog Fennel has classic daisy-like flowers with yellow centers and **white petals**.

GETTING RID OF IT!

Tansy spreads by rhizomes, and even small pieces will produce a new plant. Persistent, repeated pulling may be effective on small patches, and will slow down reproduction if the plants are pulled before the seedheads develop. Wear gloves when pulling tansy, as it may cause dermatitis.

WHAT'S IT GOOD FOR?

Tansy has been used medicinally, to treat conditions ranging from parasites to migraines. It is generally no longer recommended for these uses, as it contains some toxic compounds that can cause problems. It repels flies and other insects, and was used in the past to keep flies off corpses prior to burial.

Canada Goldenrod   *(Solidago canadensis, S. altissima)*

OVERVIEW: Two native Goldenrods that are common in our region are both called Canada Goldenrod. Some sources consider *S. altissima* to be a subspecies of *S. canadensis*; others consider the two as separate species. They are very difficult to separate visually, and are treated jointly here. Canada Goldenrod is a native perennial that is 2 to 6 feet tall. The stem is unbranched and round, with faint lines of white hairs along the length. Canada Goldenrod often grows in dense colonies.

WHERE YOU'LL FIND IT: Sunny areas with moderate soil moisture. It is found in both disturbed and natural areas, including hills along walking trails, edges of urban parks, thickets, limestone glades, fields, vacant lots, savannas and waste ground. It is common throughout our region.

LEAVES: The **lance-like** leaves grow alternately, on very short stalks or attached directly to the stem (sessile). Leaves are up to 6 inches long, and usually have small teeth around the edges. The midrib is fairly prominent; 2 curved veins that are slightly shallower flank it on either side.

FLOWERS/FRUIT: **Plume-like spikes** of bright golden-yellow flowers grow sideways from the top of the plant; the spikes typically **arch gracefully** and the flowers grow only on one side of the spike. Each flowerhead consists of numerous narrow ray florets held in a cuplike base. The flowerheads are about ¼ inch across; when *S. canadensis* and *S. altissima* are compared, the flowers of *S. canadensis* will be smaller.

SEASON: Flowers are present from midsummer into fall.

OTHER NAMES: Some sources refer to *S. altissima* as Late Goldenrod or Tall Goldenrod.

COMPARE: Giant Goldenrod (*S. gigantea*; also called Smooth Goldenrod) is another native perennial that is found throughout our area. Stems are up to **7 feet** tall and light green to **purplish or reddish**; they are **hairless** and somewhat **waxy**. It may bloom slightly earlier than Canada Goldenrod, but this is variable.

GETTING RID OF IT!

Mowing in late spring and late summer will help control Goldenrods, but will not eliminate them because they spread by rhizomes that continue to produce new plants. Pulling will diminish small infestations, but needs to be repeated frequently as new plants sprout.

WHAT'S IT GOOD FOR?

Honey made by bees that have been feeding primarily on Goldenrod is golden and mildly spicy. Contrary to common belief, Goldenrod flowers are not the cause of hayfever and other allergies; you can blame that on Ragweeds (pgs. 56 and 58). Current research suggests that Goldenrod compounds might be able to fight antibiotic-resistant bacterial strains.

Tall Beggar's Ticks

(Bidens vulgata)

OVERVIEW: This native annual wildflower is often considered weedy because its flowers are not particularly showy and it often spreads to areas where it's not wanted. It reportedly can be up to 6 feet tall, but is more commonly 2 to 4 feet. Stems are smooth at the base and moderately hairy above; they branch repeatedly, so plants look rather bushy.

WHERE YOU'LL FIND IT: Disturbed areas with full sun to moderate shade, including ditches, parking lot edges, open woods, waste areas and path edges. In our region, it is scattered in all states, although it is mostly absent from northern Michigan and much of Ohio.

LEAVES: **Compound leaves with 3 to 5 leaflets** are up to 10 inches long near the base of the plant, becoming smaller towards the top; they grow oppositely on long stalks. Leaflets are bright green and **lance-like**, with pointed tips and toothy edges; they have a **prominent central vein** and numerous straight side veins, and are up to 3 inches long on larger leaves. Small, non-compound leaves are often present near the flowers.

FLOWERS/FRUIT: The **dull yellow flowerhead** is up to 1 inch across, composed of many tiny disk florets and, usually, a few small petal-like ray florets. **Eleven to 20 oblong, leaflike green bracts** grow at the flowerhead's base. Flat, oblong brownish-green seeds up to ¼ inch long replace the flowers; the top edges of the seeds have **2 slender, sharp hook-like projections** (called awns) on the outside corners that catch in clothing and animal fur, helping to spread the plants.

SEASON: Flowers bloom from late summer to fall.

OTHER NAMES: Big Devil's Beggarticks.

COMPARE: Common Beggar's Ticks (*B. frondosa*; also called Devil's Beggar Ticks) is very similar, but it has **10 or fewer** leafy green bracts surrounding the yellow flowerhead. Plants are 3 feet tall or shorter. This native annual is found in about the same portions of our area as Tall Beggar's Ticks, although may be more common in some areas.

GETTING RID OF IT!

Both Beggar's Ticks discussed here have short taproots with thin side rootlets, and are easy to pull when the soil is moist. They reproduce by seed, so the plants should be removed before seeds develop.

WHAT'S IT GOOD FOR?

The flowers are not particularly attractive to most insects, although bees will visit occasionally. There seem to be no medicinal or culinary uses for Beggar's Ticks.

Orange Hawkweed

(Hieracium aurantiacum)

OVERVIEW: Pretty flowers notwithstanding, this non-native perennial has become an invasive pest. Plants are typically 10 to 20 inches tall; flowers grow atop a **hairy** stem that is typically **leafless** and arises from a **basal cluster of hairy leaves**. Stems emit **milky juice** when broken.

WHERE YOU'LL FIND IT: Sunny to lightly shaded areas, with moderate soil moisture. Orange Hawkweed is a colonizer of disturbed places, and flourishes in waste areas and fallow fields, along roads and railroads, and in pastures. It also grows in rocky places, on streambanks and along shorelines, and can invade lawns and gardens. In our region, it is prevalent around the Great Lakes, and grows throughout Wisconsin and Michigan, in the eastern half of Minnesota, and in eastern Ohio.

LEAVES: Oblong, untoothed, **very hairy** leaves, typically 2 to 5 inches long with a rounded to softly pointed tip, grow in a **basal cluster**. One or 2 smaller leaves may grow alternately on the lower part of the stem.

FLOWERS/FRUIT: Dandelion-like flowers, ¾ to **1 inch** across, grow in **clusters of up to a dozen** on short, hairy stalks at the stem tops; only a few flowers are open in each cluster at the same time. The petal-like ray florets are numerous and reddish-orange, **deep orange** to orangish-yellow with **square tips**; the flower's center is paler. Each flower produces up to 30 long, tiny seeds that have fluffy pale hairs.

SEASON: Flowers are present from early summer through early fall.

OTHER NAMES: Devil's Paintbrush, King Devil.

COMPARE: Meadow Hawkweed (*H. caespitosum*; also called Field Hawkweed) is a similar, related non-native perennial that can also be invasive. Its flowers are similar to those of Orange Hawkweed but are **yellow** and smaller, generally ¾ inch across or less; clusters may contain **25 or more flowers**. Basal leaves may be up to **10 inches** long, and the stem may be up to **3 feet** in height. In our region, it is found in the same areas as Orange Hawkweed but is less common.

Orange Hawkweed

Meadow Hawkweed

GETTING RID OF IT!

The Hawkweeds discussed here reproduce by seed; they also have underground rhizomes and surface runners (stolons), and new plants can develop from even small fragments of either. Hand-pulling when the soil is moist works for small infestations, but the entire root system must be removed. Mowing is not recommended because it will distribute the stolons, producing more plants. Strong chemicals, such as glyphosate, may be the best solution for large patches.

WHAT'S IT GOOD FOR?

Bees and butterflies visit the plants; songbirds and upland birds eat the seeds. The foliage is bitter, but will be browsed occasionally by wildlife.

Common Mallow

(Malva neglecta)

OVERVIEW: Looking like Ground Ivy (pg. 52) on steroids, this non-native annual has sturdy, branching green stems up to 3 feet long, but they usually sprawl sideways. Leaf stalks and side branches are more likely to stand upright, giving the plant a height of 6 to 12 inches.

WHERE YOU'LL FIND IT: Edges of lawns and gardens, planted boulevards, roadsides, vacant lots, fencelines, sidewalk edges, old fields and along culverts. It prefers sun and moderately moist soil. It is found throughout our region, although it is less reported in the northwest quarter.

LEAVES: **Kidney-shaped to nearly round leaves**, 1 to 3 inches wide, grow alternately on finely hairy stalks up to **3 inches long**. Leaf edges are **scalloped** and have 5 or more shallow lobes; the base is deeply cleft where it attaches to the stalk. The top surface may be smooth or have scattered hairs; the underside is hairy.

FLOWERS/FRUIT: Five-petaled **pinkish** to white flowers, ¼ to **½ inch across**, grow in small clusters on thin 1-inch stalks from leaf axils. Petals have blunt edges that are slightly notched or wavy; faint pinkish stripes run from the center to the edge. Flowers are replaced by circular, flattened, **smooth** green seedpods that are ¼ inch across and nestled in a cup of leaflike green sepals. They somewhat resemble **small wheels of cheese**, and are commonly called "cheeses" by foragers.

SEASON: Common Mallow is in bloom continuously from mid-spring through fall. Fruits develop from early summer through fall.

OTHER NAMES: Buttonweed, Cheeseweed, Cheeseplant.

COMPARE: Dwarf Mallow (*M. pusilla*; also called *M. rotundifolia* and Round-Leaved Mallow) is very similar, but its flowers are just ¼ inch across and typically white. The green, hairy leaflike sepals, which are hidden behind the petals of Common Mallow, are **visible behind the petals** of Dwarf Mallow. The cheeses have a **rough** surface. Dwarf Mallow is less common in our region.

Common Mallow (all 3)

GETTING RID OF IT!

Unlike Ground Ivy, Mallow stems do not root at the nodes. Common and Dwarf Mallows reproduce by seed, so they should be removed before they flower (which is continuous throughout the summer). Pulling is effective as long as the entire tap root is removed. Frequent mowing at low heights will also help control Mallow.

WHAT'S IT GOOD FOR?

When green, the raw cheeses are sweet and somewhat sticky; children particularly enjoy them. Young leaves are edible raw or cooked, and the cheeses can also be cooked; all parts release thickening mucilage during cooking and can be used to thicken soups and stews, much like okra.

Lady's Thumb

(Persicaria maculosa)

OVERVIEW: This non-native annual is typically 1 to 2 feet tall; it usually stands upright but longer stems may sprawl sideways. Stems are round and light green or reddish; upper branches may be lightly hairy.

WHERE YOU'LL FIND IT: Favors disturbed areas in sun to partial shade, and requires adequate moisture. It is a common urban weed that grows in alleys, along roads, on the edges of parking lots, next to buildings and in vacant lots. It is also found in weedy meadows, marshy areas, ditches and along the margins of cultivated fields. It is common throughout most of our area except the Dakotas, where it is scattered.

LEAVES: Lance-like leaves, typically 2 to 4 inches long, grow alternately on short stalks or attached directly to the stem (sessile). Most leaves have a **dark oval to triangular spot** that looks like the imprint of a thumb. A **thin, ribbed sheath** called an ocrea wraps around the leaf node. The ocrea extends up the stem above the leaf base, becoming translucent; several **short, hairlike bristles** grow from the ocrea's top.

FLOWERS/FRUIT: Tiny, **bud-like** flowers are densely packed on spikelike racemes (pg. 17) that are typically **1 to 1½ inches** long and stand **upright** at the tops of stems; smaller spikes also grow from leaf axils. Flowers are **whitish, pale pink or deep rose**; colors may be mixed on each raceme. Each flower is replaced by a flattened, oval seed.

SEASON: Lady's Thumb blooms from late spring into early fall.

OTHER NAMES: Spotted Ladysthumb, Smartweed, *Polygonum persicaria.*

COMPARE: Two native annual species are similar, but their leaves typically have no spots and their ocreas **lack bristles** at the top. • Racemes of Nodding or Pale Smartweed (*P. lapathifolia;* found throughout our area) are **4 or more inches** long and **arched**; flowers are **whitish-green to white**. Plants are up to **4 feet** tall. • Racemes of Pennsylvania Smartweed (*P. pensylvanica*; range similar to Lady's Thumb) are up to **2 inches** long and **upright**; flowers are white or pale pink. Plants are up to 3 feet tall.

Lady's Thumb flowers

Lady's Thumb ocrea

Lady's Thumb

Nodding Smartweed

GETTING RID OF IT!

Lady's Thumb and the related plants discussed here spread by seed only. They have shallow root systems, making the plants easy to pull, and you don't have to worry about root fragments resprouting.

WHAT'S IT GOOD FOR?

Flowers of Smartweeds (including Lady's Thumb) attract bees, butter-flies and other insects. The seeds are eaten by many birds, including songbirds, upland birds, and waterfowl when the plants are growing in wet areas. Foliage is bitter and unappealing to most browsing mammals.

Motherwort

(Leonurus cardiaca)

OVERVIEW: A non-native perennial, Motherwort is typically 2 to 4 feet tall and usually unbranched. The stem is **square** and **ridged**, with scattered fine hairs. It frequently grows in colonies that can become fairly large.

WHERE YOU'LL FIND IT: Motherwort prefers lightly shaded areas with rich, moist soil, including open woodlands, swamp edges and scrubby areas next to vacant fields. In populated areas, it grows along paths and roads, and in dumps, disturbed sites, city parks and landscaped areas. It is found in every state of our region, but is sparse to absent in the Dakotas and the northern parts of Minnesota, Wisconsin and Michigan.

LEAVES: Dull green leaves with fairly deep **netlike veins** grow oppositely on long stalks. Leaves near the base have **3 to 5 deep lobes**, each with large, coarse teeth; they have wide bases and look like **wrinkled maple leaves**. Leaves become smaller and simpler as they ascend the stem; most of the stem leaves on a mature plant are elliptic, with **tapered bases** and **3 pointed lobes** with a few shallow, wide teeth; at the top, leaves are typically unlobed, with pointed tips. Sizes range from nearly 5 inches long for the lower leaves, to 2 inches long at the top of the plant.

FLOWERS/FRUIT: Very **hairy**, pinkish to lavender **2-lipped flowers** grow in clusters at leaf nodes on the upper stem. Flowers are about ⅓ inch across and are **attached directly to the stem**. They are replaced by brown seed capsules that have multiple sharp points.

SEASON: Flowers bloom from early to midsummer. The brown capsules appear in late summer, and remain on the leafless stalk into winter.

OTHER NAMES: Common Motherwort, Throw-Wort, Lion's Ear, Lion's Tail.

COMPARE: Wild Mint (*Mentha arvensis*) has square stems with flowers in its leaf axils, but leaves are **oval** and **unlobed**, with toothy edges. Flowers are pink, lavender or whitish, and have **several lobes**; **stamens protrude beyond the petals**. All parts of the plant **smell like mint** when crushed. It grows throughout our area except the far south.

Motherwort | Wild Mint

GETTING RID OF IT!

Motherwort spreads by seeds as well as by spreading rhizomes and is considered invasive in many areas. Small patches can be pulled before the plants go to seed; root fragments left behind will resprout, requiring additional work. Triclopyr or glyphosate are needed for large infestations.

WHAT'S IT GOOD FOR?

Motherwort has been used as a medicinal herb in Europe, Asia and North America for centuries. In the "language of flowers" dating to Victorian times, a bouquet of Motherwort signified concealed love. Bees seem to love the plant; long-tongued bees such as bumblebees collect the nectar, in turn pollinating the plants.

Crown Vetch

(Securigera varia)

OVERVIEW: Variously described as a vine, a ground cover and an upright plant, this non-native perennial has characteristics of all three. It has weak, spreading stems growing from a woody base called a caudex. Upright flowering stems may stand up to 3 feet tall, particularly when they have a support to lean on, but are generally shorter; trailing stems can be 6 feet long. Stems are green and hairless or sparsely hairy. Mature stems are thick and **ridged**; young growth and floral stems are thin and wiry. Crown Vetch forms **dense mats** that crowd out other plants.

WHERE YOU'LL FIND IT: Widely planted for erosion control, Crown Vetch has taken over roadsides and freeway embankments in those areas. It also grows along ditches, on riverbanks and in meadows. It is still sold as a garden ornamental, and has escaped into neighboring gardens as well as parks and nearby wooded areas. In our region, it is fairly common in Minnesota, southeastern Wisconsin, much of Illinois and all of Indiana. It is scattered in Iowa, Michigan, Ohio and South Dakota.

LEAVES: Compound leaves with **11 to 25** oblong leaflets grow alternately. Leaves are typically 2 to 4 inches long, but may be longer.

FLOWERS/FRUIT: Five to 25 **pea-like** flowers, each about ½ inch long, grow in **rounded 1-inch clusters** on **long, leafless** stems arising from leaf axils. Flowers are combinations of deep rose, pale pink, white and lavender. Fruits are long, thin pods up to 2 inches long that grow in clusters; they look like **green beans** with a thin brown tail at the end.

SEASON: Flowers bloom in profusion from early to late summer.

OTHER NAMES: Trailing Crownvetch, *Coronilla varia*.

COMPARE: Common Vetch (*Vicia sativa*; non-native) is an annual with **sparse**, pink pea-like flowers that grow **singly or in pairs;** they grow from leaf axils and have virtually **no stalk**. The compound leaves have 11 to 13 oblong leaflets. Seedpods look like **snow peas**. It is sparsely scattered throughout our region and is fairly common in Wisconsin.

GETTING RID OF IT!

Crown Vetch has a strong root system, with a thick, deep taproot and branching rhizomes that grow up to 10 feet per year. Digging out the root system of a well-developed patch is nearly impossible. You may try to tackle a small patch, but repeat digging will be required as any broken-off rhizomes will continue to sprout. Mowing in early summer, and again in late summer, will tamp down but not eliminate colonies of Crown Vetch.

WHAT'S IT GOOD FOR?

Crown Vetch has attractive flowers, and it's easy to understand why it has been planted as an ornamental. However, we are now aware of its invasive potential.

Wild Four o'Clock

(Mirabilis nyctaginea)

OVERVIEW: You may see this native perennial frequently if you live in an urban area, but chances are good that you've never noticed its flowers, which are small and closed most of the day. Plants branch repeatedly, particularly at the top, and are typically 2 to 3 feet tall, but may be 4 feet. Stems are smooth and green, with white stripes; they are angular at the plant's base, becoming rounded at the top. Leaf nodes may be reddish.

WHERE YOU'LL FIND IT: Sunny, dry spots, typically with poor soil; it thrives in disturbed areas. In urban areas, it grows along sidewalks and alleys, in junkyards and abandoned lots, and next to lamp posts, athletic fields and buildings. It is also found in prairies, pastures, fallow fields, and in rocky areas along railroads and ditches. It grows throughout our region, although it is less common in Michigan, Ohio and South Dakota.

LEAVES: Smooth, **egg- to heart-shaped** leaves up to 4 inches long grow oppositely on short stalks. Leaf edges are untoothed and often wavy.

FLOWERS/FRUIT: Bright magenta or pinkish-purple flowers, ½ inch across, grow in small, tight clusters at the ends of branching stems; they are contained in a 5-sided leaflike green bract. Flowers have 5 petal-like sepals that are fused at the base; the tips are notched, so the flowers look somewhat **ruffled**. Several long, pink stamens with yellow tips project beyond the sepals. They **open in late afternoon** and **close the following morning**, usually early. The bracts eventually dry out, becoming papery; dry seeds are clustered in the center.

SEASON: Flowers are present from early to late summer.

OTHER NAMES: Heartleaf Four o'Clock, Umbrella Wort.

COMPARE: Hairy Four o'Clock (*M. albida*; also called White Four o'Clock) has similarly shaped flowers, but they are **white to pale pink**. Leaves are **long and narrow**, and grow primarily at the base of the plant. All parts of the plant are **densely hairy**. It is less common than Wild Four o'Clock; in our region it is found primarily in the western half.

GETTING RID OF IT!

Wild Four o'Clock reproduces by seed. Young plants are easy to pull when the soil is moist. Older plants develop a large, fleshy taproot that can be a foot or more long, so pulling is ineffective because the woody stems break off at the ground, leaving the roots in the soil. Digging is the best solution for small patches. Large infestations can be mowed frequently to reduce plant vigor and prevent seeds from developing. The plants are resistant to some herbicides.

WHAT'S IT GOOD FOR?

Native peoples including the Oglala Sioux used a tea made from the roots to control fever; the tea was also used externally to heal sores.

Common Milkweed

(Asclepias syriaca)

OVERVIEW: Although many milkweed species grow in our region, this is the one that is most familiar, and is usually referred to simply as Milkweed. It is a native perennial whose **straight, stout stem** is round, pale green and **downy**; it is typically unbranched, although some plants branch at the top. Common Milkweed can be up to 6 feet tall. All parts of the plant produce **milky sap** when broken; the sap can irritate skin.

WHERE YOU'LL FIND IT: Milkweed prefers rich, moist soil with full sun, but adapts to a variety of situations. It grows in gardens and landscaped areas, next to buildings and fences, in vacant lots, and along roads and railroads; it's also found in prairies, on sandy dunes, and on edges of fields and woodlands. It grows in the northeastern quarter of the U.S., and is common throughout our area except the western half of the Dakotas.

LEAVES: **Oblong** leaves, up to 8 inches long and a third as wide, grow oppositely on stubby stalks. Leaves are deep green and smooth above, with smooth edges that are often **wavy**; undersides are covered with short, wooly hairs that give them a **pale green** appearance.

FLOWERS/FRUIT: **Round clusters** of flowers grow on stemlets arising from leaf axils in the upper part of the plant; clusters are typically 2 to 3 inches across. Flowers are ¼ inch wide and **pink to pale purplish**, with 5 petals; they grow on **long, thin stemlets** that are all **attached to a central point**, like the spokes of an umbrella (umbellate) and typically droop downward. A few flowers in each cluster develop into **bumpy, pale green pods** that are 3 to 5 inches long with **swollen** bases. The pods split open to release brown seeds that have white hairlike tufts.

SEASON: Flowers are present from early to late summer; pods split in fall.

OTHER NAMES: Silkweed, Showy Milkweed.

COMPARE: Poke Milkweed (*A. exaltata*) looks very similar to Common Milkweed, but its flowers are **white** and its pods are **very narrow**. In our region, it is scattered throughout the eastern two-thirds.

GETTING RID OF IT!

Milkweeds are essential to Monarch butterflies (see below), and should be removed only when they're really in the way. They are easy to pull when the soil is moist; wear gloves to avoid the sap, and pull straight up.

WHAT'S IT GOOD FOR?

Common Milkweed and other Milkweeds are the *only* food source for the larvae of Monarch butterflies, and the plant's presence is key to the Monarch's survival. Milkweed populations have been declining severely due to habitat loss and land development, and the future of the Monarch is in jeopardy. Look up the many *Asclepias* species in a wildflower book or online, and consider planting some in your garden.

Canada Thistle

(Cirsium arvense)

OVERVIEW: Often found in large colonies, this non-native perennial is up to 5 feet tall; the top half typically branches into numerous side stems. Stems are **ridged and greenish**, sometimes with a reddish tint; there may be sparse hairs on the stems but there are **no spines**.

WHERE YOU'LL FIND IT: Sunny areas, including ditches, meadows, grassy strips next to parking lots, railroad embankments and poorly kept lawns. Canada Thistle is common throughout our region except in southern Illinois. It is listed as a noxious weed in all states of our region.

LEAVES: **Glossy** leaves that appear somewhat **curled** grow alternately, with no stalk (sessile); **both surfaces are green**. Edges are wavy and have **numerous small spines**. Leaves towards the base are up to 7 inches long and half as wide, with **distinct lobes**. Towards the top, leaves become smaller, **elliptic and unlobed**, with large, irregular teeth.

FLOWERS/FRUIT: Flowers that are ½ to ¾ inch across grow at the tops of the stems, singly or in small clusters. The base (called the involucre) is **teardrop-shaped** and covered with **flat, overlapping greenish scalelike bracts with pointed purplish tips**. A spray of slender pale pink or lavender florets grows upward from the involucre. Each floret is replaced by a seed with a tan to white tuft of hair (called a pappus).

SEASON: Flowers are typically present from early to late summer.

OTHER NAMES: Field Thistle, a name that is also used for *C. discolor*, below.

COMPARE: Field Thistle (*C. discolor*; native perennial) is more scattered throughout our region; it is not found in the Dakotas. Like Canada Thistle, its stems are non-spiny, but they may be up to **7 feet tall**. The scalelike bracts on its involucre have **vertical white stripes; thin, soft spines project outward** from the bract tips. Several **long, thin bracts curl around the base of the involucre**. All leaves are deeply lobed and have spines at the lobe tips; **leaf undersides are white**. Flowers are up to **2 inches across**. It begins blooming a bit later than Canada Thistle.

Canada Thistle
(above and left)

Field Thistle (2 above,
and unopened
flower, right)

GETTING RID OF IT!

These two thistles reproduce by seed as well as rhizomes. Mowing prior to flowering will prevent seed formation, but the rhizomes will send up new shoots. Attempts to dig it out break up the rhizomes, and even small pieces produce new plants. Repeated, frequent pulling or removal with a dandelion prong will slowly pay off, but it requires persistence. If you resort to glyphosate, use a light application, allowing the chemical to be absorbed into the roots rather than simply killing the leaves.

WHAT'S IT GOOD FOR?

Songbirds eat the seeds of both thistles listed here. Bees, butterflies and other insects visit the plants for nectar and pollen.

Common Burdock

(Arctium minus)

OVERVIEW: This non-native plant is a biennial whose first-year rosettes strongly **resemble garden rhubarb**. In its second year, plants produce stout, brittle stems up to 6 feet tall that branch near the top. Stems are pale green and usually downy; they are round and somewhat ribbed. **Thistle-like flowers** grow in profusion towards the top of the plant.

WHERE YOU'LL FIND IT: Full sun to moderately heavy shade, in a variety of soil types and moisture levels. It is common along paths in wooded areas and parks, and flourishes in scrubby areas next to roads, fences and parking lots; it is also found in waste areas, open woodlands, pastures and ditches. It is common throughout our region, although it is less reported in South Dakota and western Ohio.

LEAVES: The basal leaves are narrowly **heart-shaped with ruffled edges**; they are up to 2 feet long and grow on long, **roundly grooved** stalks. Stem leaves of second-year plants become smaller and less ruffled as they ascend the stem; the leaf stalks are short or absent. All leaves are dull green above, with **pale green, downy undersides**.

FLOWERS/FRUIT: Flowers up to ¾ **inch wide** grow at the tops of the stems, singly or in small clusters. The base is **rounded** and covered with narrow, spiny bracts that have **hooked tips**. A cap of slender pinkish to purplish florets grows upward from the base. Seeds develop from the florets and the bracts turn brown, curling in to enclose the seeds; the resulting bur commonly hooks onto clothing and animal hair.

SEASON: Common Burdock flowers from midsummer to early fall.

OTHER NAMES: Lesser Burdock, Wild Rhubarb.

COMPARE: Great Burdock (*A. lappa*; non-native biennial) may be up to 9 feet in height, and its flowering heads are up to **1½ inches** across. It is sometimes grown as a root vegetable and occasionally escapes cultivation to become a noxious weed. In our region it is reported in all states but it is uncommon and distribution is scattered.

GETTING RID OF IT!

Common Burdock spreads by seed, and can form colonies. First-year plants have a deep taproot that can be dug out, but it is a tedious job; glyphosate is effective if sprayed on the leaves. Second-year plants can be mowed prior to flowering; the roots can resprout and produce more flowers, so a second mowing may be required. For small numbers of second-year plants, use a sharp, narrow spade or other sharp tool to sever the root several inches below the soil, then pull out the stem.

WHAT'S IT GOOD FOR?

Dried roots, primarily from Great Burdock but also from Common Burdock, are used medicinally. Fresh roots are edible when cooked.

Bull Thistle

(Cirsium vulgare)

OVERVIEW: This non-native thistle grows to 6 feet in height. It is **very spiny** overall. The thick stem is ribbed or angular and **covered with white hairs**; spiny wings grow down the stem from leaf bases and also over other parts of the stem. It is biennial, flowering in its second year.

WHERE YOU'LL FIND IT: Alleys, meadows, roadsides, trail edges, railroad embankments and waste ground. Found throughout the U.S.; classified as noxious in Indiana, Iowa, Michigan, Minnesota and South Dakota.

LEAVES: A large rosette of spiny basal leaves grows the first year. A stem with alternate leaves up to 6 inches long develops in the second year. Leaves have deeply cut **narrow lobes** with a long, pale yellowish spine at the tip of each lobe. The top surface is deep green and rough, with fine hairs; the lower surface appears **wooly**.

FLOWERS/FRUIT: The flowerhead is up to 2 inches wide. The base (called the involucre) is **vase-shaped** and covered with narrow, spine-tipped bracts that **curve outward**. A dense cap of slender, deep pink to purplish florets grows upward from the involucre. Each floret is replaced by a seed with a feathery white tuft of hair (called a pappus).

SEASON: Flowers are present from midsummer through early fall.

OTHER NAMES: Spear Thistle, Black Thistle.

COMPARE: Nodding Thistle (*Carduus nutans*; non-native biennial) has triangular **reddish-purple bracts** projecting from its **cup-shaped** involucre. Flowerheads are up to **3 inches across** and often droop sideways when mature. **Stem are spineless** for a few inches under the flowers, but typically densely spiny elsewhere. It is scattered in all states of our region, and listed as noxious in most. • Plumeless Thistle (*Carduus acanthoides*; non-native biennial) has a **cup-shaped** involucre that is **covered in thin, spiny bracts** that curve outward. Flowerheads are **1 inch wide or less**. Stems have spiny wings **over their entire length**. In our region it is found mostly in Minnesota and western Iowa.

Nodding Thistle

Bull Thistle (all)   Plumeless Thistle

GETTING RID OF IT!

The thistles listed here reproduce by seed, so cutting down second-year plants prior to flowering will help control them. If flowers have developed, cut down the stems and destroy the flowerheads to prevent them from forming seeds, which they may do even after being cut off. Dig out several inches of the root after cutting the stems, to prevent regrowth. Rosettes can be sprayed in the fall with triclopyr or metsulfuron.

WHAT'S IT GOOD FOR?

Hummingbirds, bees and butterflies sip thistle nectar. Goldfinches and other songbirds eat the seeds, and goldfinches line their nests with the seed plumes.

Catnip

(Nepeta cataria)

OVERVIEW: Yes, this is the same plant whose leaves are used in cat toys. This non-native perennial usually stands 1 to 2 feet tall, although it can grow to 4 feet if left unchecked. It is a member of the mint family and has the **square** stems typical of that group; stems of Catnip are **downy** and usually greenish, but may have a reddish cast. Catnip branches near the top and can be fairly bushy. It often grows in colonies.

WHERE YOU'LL FIND IT: Grows in full sun to moderate shade. It does well in disturbed areas and is often found along railroad tracks and gravel roads, but also grows in weedy fields, open deciduous woodlands, gardens and park edges. It is found in all states of our area, although it is largely absent from the northern parts of South Dakota, Minnesota and Wisconsin, and the southern parts of Illinois and Indiana.

LEAVES: Egg-shaped to heart-shaped leaves grow oppositely on short, **downy** stalks; edges have **rounded teeth** all around. Leaves are 1 to 3 inches long; they are **downy** on both surfaces and have fairly **deep veins**, often appearing somewhat wrinkled and dusty. When bruised, they have a **strong, herbal scent**.

FLOWERS/FRUIT: A dense, whorled cluster of pinkish or whitish flowers grows as a spikelike raceme (pg. 17) at the tops of the stems; short racemes may also grow from leaf axils. Flowers are up to ½ inch long, and have **2 lobed lips** that open up from a tubular base. The lower lip has **purplish dots and markings** inside. A hairy green base surrounds the tube; the outer surfaces of the flowers are similarly **hairy**. The fruit is a brown, urn-like capsule.

SEASON: Catnip is in flower from midsummer through early fall.

OTHER NAMES: Catweed, Cat Mint.

COMPARE: American Germander (*Teucrium canadense*) has tall racemes of white to pale lavender flowers up to ¾ inch long; its leaves are **lance-like**. This native perennial grows in all states of our region.

GETTING RID OF IT!

Although your cat may enjoy having this plant in your yard, you might find it difficult to eradicate once it becomes established. It spreads by seeds and rhizomes. If you want to keep a small patch for your cat, be sure to cut off flowerheads before they go to seed, and pull out small seedlings as they appear. Larger or unwanted patches should be dug out.

WHAT'S IT GOOD FOR?

Tea made from catnip leaves that have been infused (not boiled) is used for headaches, and also as a mild sedative and stress-reducer. It is also used as a natural insect repellent. Cats become pretty silly when playing with catnip toys, although it may simply make them fall asleep.

Spotted Knapweed

(Centaurea stoebe)

OVERVIEW: This non-native weed is a biennial that becomes a short-lived perennial. First-year growth is a basal rosette; the plants that develop the following year usually survive 3 to 7 years. Stems are typically 2 to 3 feet high; they are ridged and **branch repeatedly**. Spotted Knapweed is highly invasive and is often seen in **massive colonies**.

WHERE YOU'LL FIND IT: Spotted Knapweed thrives in sunny spots like meadows, prairies, waste areas, scrubby parks and along roads and railroads, but it also grows in areas that are shaded part of the day, such as next to buildings. It is present in all states of our area but is most common in Minnesota, Wisconsin and Michigan.

LEAVES: Deeply lobed leaves with numerous **narrow segments** grow on long stalks in the basal rosette; they are up to 8 inches long and **grayish-green** with a dusty appearance. Leaves on the bottom parts of the stems are shorter, stalkless and less lobed, becoming progressively shorter as they ascend the stems; leaves near the flowers are **linear and unlobed**. Stem leaves grow alternately.

FLOWERS/FRUIT: Flowers grow singly at the tops of the stems, and from stemlets originating in leaf axils. The **teardrop-shaped** base is covered with **flat, overlapping green scalelike bracts with dark brown tips;** the tips have **coarse hairs** around the edge. A loose spray of slender purplish florets grows from the base; flowerheads are about 1 inch wide. Each flower is replaced by a seed with a tuft of bristles.

SEASON: Flowers are present from summer through early fall.

OTHER NAMES: *C. stoebe* ssp. *micranthos, C. maculosa*.

COMPARE: Spotted Knapweed flowers resemble those of Canada Thistle (pg. 160), but leaves of Canada Thistle are **elliptic**, with **prickles** around the edges. • Russian Knapweed (*Rhaponticum repens* or *C. repens*; non-native) has similar flowers, but the bracts are **rounded and translucent**. In our area it grows in the Dakotas and western Minnesota.

Large infestation of Spotted Knapweed

GETTING RID OF IT!

Spotted Knapweed reproduces by seeds that remain viable in the soil for up to 7 years. It can take some time to stamp down an infestation, as new plants grow from the stored seeds and also from buds on the root crowns of the previous year's plants. Plants can be pulled when the soil is moist; a shovel may be needed to remove the taproot of older plants. Some people have an allergic reaction when handling the plants; wear long sleeves and gloves, and dispose of all flowerheads in plastic bags.

WHAT'S IT GOOD FOR?

Bees that sip nectar from the flowers of Spotted Knapweed produce very flavorful honey.

Purple Loosestrife
(Lythrum salicaria)

OVERVIEW: Although this book does not discuss aquatic weeds, Purple Loosestrife is included because it is highly invasive and may be found encroaching on habitable areas. In our region, this non-native perennial is typically up to 6 feet tall and branches frequently below the flowering spikes. Stems are square, greenish and fuzzy in the upper parts, becoming woody and smooth near the base. In our region, it is most common in the northern half, and is also common in much of Ohio.

WHERE YOU'LL FIND IT: Sunny wetland areas. It grows in dense stands around the edges of lakes, rivers and streams, and can also survive in deep ditches; it is increasingly seen along major highways. Purple Loosestrife spreads rampantly and can take over shallow marshes and fens. In habitable areas it grows in landscaped locations abutting water features. It is found throughout our area but is most common in Minnesota, Wisconsin, Michigan, northern Indiana and Ohio; it is listed as a noxious weed in all states in our region except Illinois.

LEAVES: Oblong to lance-like leaves up to 4 inches long, with pointed tips and rounded bases, grow **oppositely**, or sometimes in whorls of several leaves. They are attached directly to the stem (sessile).

FLOWERS/FRUIT: Bright **pink or pinkish-purple** flowers grow densely packed on a **floral spike up to 2 feet long** at the top of each stem; small pointed leaves are scattered along the spike. Flowers are ½ to ¾ inch across and have 5 to 7 oblong petals. The fruit is a small, oblong capsule containing about a hundred seeds.

SEASON: Flowers are present from midsummer to early fall.

OTHER NAMES: Spiked Loosestrife, *L. palustre.*

COMPARE: Fireweed (*Epilobium angustifolium*; also called *Chamerion angustifolium*) is a tall plant with a spike of purple flowers, but it grows **in soil**, not in wetlands. Its lance-like leaves are **alternate** and up to **8 inches** long. In our area, it is found primarily in the northern half.

GETTING RID OF IT!

Hand pulling can be effective for small clusters; be sure to remove the roots to prevent resprouting. If you have a large infestation, contact your local natural-resources agency to learn which methods of chemical control are allowed, and how to apply them; a permit may be required for plants that are in or near the water.

WHAT'S IT GOOD FOR?

Nothing, when compared to its invasive potential. Although it has attractive flowers, provides habitat for some birds, and is visited by bees and butterflies, this plant should be eradicated wherever it grows.

Creeping Bellflower *(Campanula rapunculoides)*

OVERVIEW: Here's another plant that was imported from Europe as an ornamental and has become invasive. It is a perennial that spreads by seeds as well as by creeping rhizomes; it often forms clumps. Stems are unbranching and up to 3 feet tall; they are green to reddish-brown.

WHERE YOU'LL FIND IT: Sunny to partially shaded areas with rich soil and adequate moisture. It is becoming increasingly common in urban areas, where it is found in alleys, next to buildings and in landscaped areas. It also grows along roads and streams, and in prairies, fields, thickets and oak savannas. Creeping Bellflower grows throughout our region; it is most common in Wisconsin, eastern Minnesota, the northern quarter of Illinois, southeastern Michigan and Michigan's Upper Peninsula.

LEAVES: Bright green, rough-textured leaves grow alternately; leaf edges are **coarsely toothed**. Leaves at the bottom of the plant are **heart-shaped** and up to 4 inches long, with stalks that are longer than the leaves. As the leaves ascend the stem they become smaller and narrower, with shorter stalks or no stalks.

FLOWERS/FRUIT: **Bell-shaped purple flowers** up to 1 inch long, with 5 petal-like lobes, grow as a loose raceme (pg. 17) at the top of the stems. They grow on **one side of the stem** only, and hang downward from short stemlets; the leaflike bracts at the base of the flowers have 5 pointed lobes that curl backwards. Fruits are round capsules.

SEASON: Flowers are most abundant in midsummer, but a few may still be present into early fall.

OTHER NAMES: Creeping Bluebell.

COMPARE: American Bellflower (*Campanula rotundifolia*; also listed as *Campanulastrum americanum*) is a native annual with a raceme of bell-shaped bluish-purple flowers that have 5 petals and a **pale lavender to cream-colored** center. Leaves are **egg-shaped to oval**, with pointed tips. In our region, it is found primarily in the northern half.

GETTING RID OF IT!

Creeping Bellflower is resistant to many herbicides; some sources say that even glyphosate doesn't work well. Pulling is ineffective because the stems break off at the ground, leaving the roots in the soil; the best solution is to dig out all of the rhizomes and the taproot, which is fairly long. Use a pitchfork to loosen the soil. Dig at least 6 inches down to get the taproot, and several inches outward from the stem to get the rhizomes. It's not a lot of fun.

WHAT'S IT GOOD FOR?

It's a pretty plant when the flowers are present, but becomes unattractive and lanky when they're gone, often falling over.

Eastern Poison Ivy

(Toxicodendron radicans)

OVERVIEW: Although this native perennial can grow as a shrub up to 3 feet tall, Eastern Poison Ivy is more typically a **vine** that can be up to 60 feet long. Stems are **woody and ropy**, and develop thick aerial **roots that attach to supporting plants or structures** with fine, dense rootlets (see small photo at right).

WHERE YOU'LL FIND IT: An adaptive plant, Eastern Poison Ivy grows in sun or shade; it prefers moist areas with good soil but tolerates drought. It is most common in open woodlands and woodland edges but also grows along fences, on trees and climbing up buildings in more habited areas. Eastern Poison Ivy is found throughout our region except the Dakotas, where it is absent or rare. It is listed as a noxious weed in Minnesota.

LEAVES: Three-part compound leaves grow on the ends of long, thin stalks attached alternately to the main stem. The **stalk of the central leaflet is longer** than those of the two side leaflets. Leaflets are egg-shaped and typically 2 to 4 inches long, occasionally longer. Edges may be smooth or have coarse, irregular teeth or wavy edges; shallow lobes are sometimes present. Leaflets turn **red** in fall.

FLOWERS/FRUIT: Flowers grow in **large, loose** clusters in leaf axils. Each is about **¼ inch across**, with 5 greenish-white triangular petals that fold backwards and 5 **brown-tipped** stamens. The **round, ridged berries** that follow are about ¼ inch across; they are greenish when immature, ripening to **dull white**. The berries are toxic.

SEASON: Plants flower from late spring to midsummer; fruits ripen in fall and may be present through winter.

OTHER NAMES: Poison Vine, *Rhus radicans*.

COMPARE: Western Poison Ivy (pg. 60) is a **tender plant** with similar leaves. Flowers are ¹⁄₁₆ inch across with **yellow-tipped** stamens, and grow in smaller clusters. Plants are typically 6 to 12 inches high, but may be up to 3 feet tall.

GETTING RID OF IT!

Never burn Poison Ivy, as the smoke it produces will cause severe respiratory distress in anyone who breathes it. Always wear gloves, long sleeves and pants when dealing with Poison Ivy; a disposable coverall is even better. Pull down the vines and cut them to ground level, transferring them to plastic bags for disposal (do not compost the plants). Dig out the roots if possible; otherwise, paint the stump with glyphosate. Rinse all tools with water, then wash with rubbing alcohol. It may take a few years to completely kill the plants.

WHAT'S IT GOOD FOR?

See the comments for Western Poison Ivy on pg. 61.

Black Bindweed

(Fallopia convolvulus)

OVERVIEW: This non-native annual has **very thin**, hairless stems that are greenish to reddish and may be up to 6 feet long but are usually shorter. Plants branch frequently near the base. The stems twine around fences, other plants and each other in a **clockwise** direction.

WHERE YOU'LL FIND IT: Most common in disturbed spots with full to partial sun. In urban areas it is found in gardens, landscaped areas, and along sidewalks and roads. It also grows in meadows, prairies and waste areas, as well as along railroad tracks. It is found throughout our area.

LEAVES: Arrowhead-shaped leaves grow alternately on moderately long, slender stalks. Leaves are up to 3 inches long and two-thirds as wide; the tips are sharply pointed and the lobes at the base are somewhat pointed. A short, papery, **hairless** sheath called an ocrea wraps around the stem at the base of each leaf; the ocrea disintegrates over time.

FLOWERS/FRUIT: Small, **bud-like** flowers grow as racemes (pg. 17) that originate in leaf axils. Flowers are ⅛ to ¼ inch long and have 3 to 5 petals or petal-like sepals that are greenish-white, white or pale pinkish. A **3-sided seed** less than ¼ inch long replaces each flower; seeds are greenish at first, ripening to **dull** black with **shiny edges**.

SEASON: Flowers develop throughout summer, maturing to seeds fairly quickly; both flowers and seeds are present most of the summer.

OTHER NAMES: Wild Buckwheat, *Polygonum convolvulus*.

COMPARE: Climbing False Buckwheat (*F. scandens*; native) is similar to Black Bindweed in general appearance, but it is a perennial vine that can grow to **20 feet** in length. Leaves are up to **4½ inches** long. The 3 outer petal-like sepals of the flower have distinct **wings**. The fruit is about **⅜ inch long** and has 3 **ruffled wings**, and the seeds are **shiny black overall**. It is found in all states of our region, but is scarce in the Dakotas, southwestern Minnesota, western Iowa and northern Michigan (including the Upper Peninsula).

Black Bindweed (main)
Black Bindweed flowers (top)
and fruits (bottom)

Climbing False
Buckwheat fruits (right)

GETTING RID OF IT!

Black Bindweed has a slender taproot and is fairly easy to pull when the plants are young. Older plants can be cut at the ground and the roots dug out. Additional pulling may be required throughout the growing season. Mowing helps control Climbing False Buckwheat; plants can also be pulled when young or dug out when older, as noted for Black Bindweed.

WHAT'S IT GOOD FOR?

The seeds are eaten by various birds and small mammals.

Five-Leaved Ivy

(Parthenocissus spp.)

OVERVIEW: Two native *Parthenocissus* species share so many of the same characteristics, it is difficult to separate them. Conflicting information has also been published about specific traits. For the homeowner, the distinctions are unimportant, so the two plants are treated here as one. For the record, the names used by the U.S.D.A are Virginia Creeper (*P. quinquefolia*) and Woodbine (*P. vitacea*, which some sources list as *P. inserta*). Both are **woody** vines that can be up to 50 feet long. They use **tendrils** to climb or otherwise attach themselves to other plants and supporting structures.

WHERE YOU'LL FIND IT: These vines are a common sight in urban areas, where they crawl up fences—particularly chain-link fences along freeways—and rough cement walls. They also grow in wooded areas and parks. Found throughout our area; Woodbine is less common.

LEAVES: Compound leaves with **5 leaflets** attached to a central point (palmate) grow on stalks up to 8 inches long. The elliptic to egg-shaped leaflets are up to 6 inches long and are bright green in summer, turning **burgundy to red** in fall. Edges have coarse teeth; tips are pointed.

FLOWERS/FRUIT: Loose clusters of ¼-inch greenish flowers grow on stemlets that originate in leaf axils. Fruits are bluish-black berries about ¼ inch across; the stemlets are **hot pink** when fruits are present.

SEASON: Flowers are present from early to midsummer; fruits ripen in fall.

COMPARE: The difference most frequently cited between these two plants is that Virginia Creeper's tendrils have **sucker feet** that attach to supporting structures or plants. Woodbine lacks these and must **coil its tendrils** around the supports. Some say that as a result of this, Woodbine is more likely to be a ground-hugging or low-growing plant because it can't climb high. • Wild grapes (*Vitis* spp.; found throughout our area) have round berries, but their leaves are **simple** (not compound), with lobes that may be shallow or distinct. Grapes have coiling tendrils that have no sucker feet, and the fruits are more **tightly clustered**.

GETTING RID OF IT!

Small plants can be pulled out, but this will have to be repeated several times each year for several years. Larger plants unfortunately require chemical treatment. Pull the vines off whatever they are clinging to without detaching them from the roots. Spread a few feet of the vine and its leaves on a sheet of plastic. Paint or spray with glyphosate or another herbicide. A few days later, cut the vine off and apply more herbicide to the cut end of the woody stump that remains.

WHAT'S IT GOOD FOR?

Juice from the dark berries was used in the past to color cheap wine. Some sources list the berries as toxic, while others say they are edible.

Japanese Hops

(Humulus japonicus)

OVERVIEW: This non-native annual vine was brought to the U.S. in the late 1800s, and began spreading vigorously on the East Coast in the 1950s. It is likely to become a serious weedy pest in our area as it continues its westward expansion. Stems are greenish to purplish and up to 20 feet long, with a **rough, bristly** texture. Although it can climb by twining around plants and other supports, it is more often seen **sprawling** on the ground, blanketing shrubs and anything else it encounters.

WHERE YOU'LL FIND IT: Sunny areas with moist, rich soil. It loves to sprawl over compost piles, and is also found crawling along riverbanks, ditches and railroad tracks; also found in weedy fields, bottomland forests and river floodplains. In our region it is scattered in the southern half; it seems particularly abundant in the counties abutting the Mississippi River and spreading out from there. It is absent from the Dakotas.

LEAVES: Dull green leaves up to 6 inches wide and long grow oppositely on stalks that may be longer than the leaves. Upper leaf surfaces are covered with **short, hooked bristles** that grab onto skin and clothing. Leaves have 5 to 7 **deeply cleft, elliptic lobes** with pointed tips; the leaf base is heart-shaped. Edges are toothy.

FLOWERS/FRUIT: Male flowers grow in **loose clusters** on floral stems up to 10 inches long. These flowers are pale green to reddish and about ⅛ inch long; they have no petals. Short spikes of female flowers grow in **short, drooping clusters on separate plants**. These flowers are pale green with **overlapping scales**; they mature into greenish "hops."

SEASON: Japanese Hops blooms from midsummer to early fall.

OTHER NAMES: *H. scandens*.

COMPARE: Common Hops (*H. lupulus*; non-native perennial) is similar, but the largest leaves have **3 broad lobes**; smaller leaves are unlobed. Scales on the hops grow more tightly together. Common Hops grows in every state of our region, and is common in Illinois, Indiana and Ohio.

GETTING RID OF IT!

Hand pulling early in the season is effective for small patches; pull when the soil is moist. The prickles on the leaves and stems can irritate or even tear the skin, so wear stout gloves when working around Japanese Hops. Cutting or mowing can be effective if started early in the season and repeated several times to prevent flowering. Large infestations, or those that can't be reached with a mower, are best handled with herbicides; consult a county agricultural agency for advice when using these chemicals near wetlands or waterways.

WHAT'S IT GOOD FOR?

Unlike Common Hops, Japanese Hops aren't used in beer making.

Hedge Bindweed

(Calystegia sepium)

OVERVIEW: A native perennial, Hedge Bindweed has round, light green to reddish stems up to 10 feet long. The stems twine around fences, shrubs and other plants in a **counterclockwise** direction, often draping over other plants until it smothers them. It is also allelopathic, producing chemicals that prevent other plants from flourishing.

WHERE YOU'LL FIND IT: Prefers moderately moist soil in full sun to part shade. It is common in urban areas, where it is seen climbing on—and over—chain-link fences, retaining walls and hedges; it also grows near wetlands, along woodland edges and in fields. It is found throughout our region, although it is less common in the Dakotas.

LEAVES: **Arrowhead-shaped** leaves, up to **5 inches** long and about half as wide, grow alternately on long, slender stalks. Leaf tips are sharply pointed. The base is notched into 2 lobes with **flat or slightly angled bases**. Edges are untoothed but often slightly hairy.

FLOWERS/FRUIT: Funnel-shaped **white to pinkish** flowers, often with ruffled edges, grow singly on long stemlets arising from leaf axils. The base of the funnel inside the flower is yellowish. Flowers are up to **2 inches** across and have 5 petals that are fused together. They open in the morning and last one day. The fruits are egg-shaped capsules.

SEASON: Plants bloom continuously from early to late summer.

OTHER NAMES: Wild Morning Glory, Giant Bindweed, *Convolvulus sepium*.

COMPARE: Field Bindweed (*Convolvulus arvensis*; non-native) appears similar to Hedge Bindweed, but its flowers are ¾ to 1 inch across and its leaves are 1 to 2 inches long. It tends to **sprawl** on the ground rather than climb. It is common throughout our region except the northern parts of Minnesota and Wisconsin, and is listed as a noxious weed in all states of our region except Illinois, Indiana and Ohio. • Common Morning Glory (pg. 188) has similar flowers that are about 2 inches across; they are typically **violet to bluish-purple**. Its leaves are **heart-shaped**.

GETTING RID OF IT!

Hedge Bindweed's roots are long but creep sideways rather than down, so it is easy to pull. Field Bindweed has deep-growing roots and is more difficult to eliminate; digging and repeated pulling will be necessary.

WHAT'S IT GOOD FOR?

According to illinoiswildflowers.info, bumblebees and other long-tongued bees are the primary pollinators of Hedge Bindweed. The foliage may be toxic to livestock when eaten in quantity. Stalks, shoots, roots and leaves are reportedly edible (by humans) when cooked.

Wild Cucumber

(Echinocystis lobata)

OVERVIEW: This native annual vine has angled, hairless stems that are 10 or more feet long. It has **forked, coiling tendrils** that it uses to climb vegetation and various supports. In late summer, you'll often see fences that are smothered in leaves with masses of white flowers at the top; if you get closer, you'll probably discover a patch of Wild Cucumber.

WHERE YOU'LL FIND IT: It prefers shady, moist areas and tends to wilt when exposed to full sun. In natural areas it is found in woodland edges, thickets and along streams. It also appears in urban areas on compost piles and other waste ground, and along freeways and roads where it climbs over fences, shrubs and small trees. In our area it is found mostly in the northern two-thirds; it is uncommon in Iowa and South Dakota.

LEAVES: The bright green, **maple-like** leaves typically have **5 triangular lobes**, but there may be as few as 3 or as many as 7. Leaves are 5 to 7 inches across and long, and grow alternately on long, thin stalks.

FLOWERS/FRUIT: Male flowers grow in **loose clusters** on 6- to 8-inch floral stemlets that originate in leaf axils. These flowers are ½ inch across, with 6 **very narrow, whitish petals** that make the flowers appear **frilly**. One to several female flowers grow on a short stemlet at the leaf axil. Female flowers have a **spiny, rounded ovary** at the base. The fertilized ovary swells into an **oval green fruit** that is 1 to 2 inches long and covered in **supple, spiny prickles**. Fruits dry out and split to release seeds.

SEASON: Plants flower in midsummer to late summer; fruits are present from late summer into early fall.

OTHER NAMES: Wild Balsam Apple, *Sicyos lobata*.

COMPARE: Bur Cucumber (*S. angulatus*; native annual) has similar leaves and growth habits, but the divisions between the leaf lobes are **more rounded and shallower**. Flowers have 5 **short, triangular green petals**. The fruit is a **many-pointed star covered with prickles**. In our region, it is scattered primarily throughout the southern half.

Bur Cucumber
fruit (right)

GETTING RID OF IT!

Small Wild Cucumber or Bur Cucumber plants should be pulled or dug out as soon as they appear. Cut stems of larger plant near ground level, before flowering. Scything or mowing can be effective for large infestations if it is done regularly and before the plants have latched onto a nearby fence or shrub.

WHAT'S IT GOOD FOR?

The roots of Wild Cucumber have been used medicinally to treat headache, stomach problems, rheumatism and even lovesickness. The seeds were used as beads by Native peoples.

Bittersweet Nightshade *(Solanum dulcamara)*

OVERVIEW: This semi-woody, non-native perennial **vine** is up to 10 feet long and often scrambles over adjacent vegetation or climbs in trees. It also sprawls along the ground, rooting at the nodes. Roots produce multiple stems, so it can spread aggressively. Stems of the current year's growth are smooth, thin and greenish-purple; older stems become woody and brown. Leaves have a **rank smell** when crushed.

WHERE YOU'LL FIND IT: Thrives in full sun but also grows in shady areas; can tolerate moderate drought. It is a common sight in urban areas, where it grows along fences and alleys, in gardens and abandoned lots, next to playgrounds and in weedy areas of parks. In rural areas it is found in meadows and woodlots, along rivers and streams, and in grassy or rocky areas around lakes. It is common throughout much of our region, but is scarce to absent in the Dakotas and western Minnesota, most of Iowa, and the southern parts of Illinois, Indiana and Ohio.

LEAVES: Bright green, glossy, egg-shaped leaves grow alternately on long, thin stalks that are slightly flattened. Many leaves have **2 ear-like lobes** at the base, and the leaf tips are pointed. Overall leaf length is up to 4 inches; the ear-like lobes span a width of up to 2½ inches.

FLOWERS/FRUIT: Star-shaped flowers grow in clusters on stemlets originating from leaf axils. Each flower is ½ inch across and has 5 **purple** petals that often curl backwards; a **bright yellow cone** projects from the center. Fruits are many-seeded berries that ripen to **glossy red**. The berries are somewhat toxic and can cause illness if eaten in quantity.

SEASON: Flowers bloom all summer; fruits ripen in late summer.

OTHER NAMES: Climbing Nightshade.

COMPARE: Black Nightshade (pg. 94) is related, but it is an **upright** plant rather than a vine. Its flowers are similar in shape to those of Bittersweet Nightshade, but they are **white**, and its ripe fruits are **black**. Its leaves **lack the ear-like lobes**.

GETTING RID OF IT!

Bittersweet Nightshade has shallow roots and is easy to pull when the soil is moist. The foliage is toxic (and smelly), so wear gloves when pulling plants. Be sure to get out all root fragments to prevent them from resprouting; digging with a hand trowel may be necessary. Never let the plants produce fruits; they will increase the spread of the plant and are somewhat toxic. Mulch over the area to prevent new growth.

WHAT'S IT GOOD FOR?

Some birds, including waterfowl, songbirds and upland birds, eat the ripe berries. (Note that although some sources list this as Deadly Nightshade, that name more properly refers to *Atropa belladonna*.)

Common Morning Glory (Ipomoea purpurea)

OVERVIEW: This non-native annual vine is planted frequently as an orna-mental, and occasionally escapes into unintended areas. Its slender round stems are tan to greenish, with a downy texture; they can be up to 10 feet long. Morning Glory climbs by **twining** its stems around fences, vegetation and other supports.

WHERE YOU'LL FIND IT: Moist areas with partial to full sun. It climbs on stop-sign posts, fences (particularly chain-link fences), and guy-wires that stabilize utility poles and radio towers. It also creeps along rocky railroad embankments and roadsides. In our region, escapees are apparently found primarily in the southern half.

LEAVES: Heart-shaped leaves up to 4 inches long and nearly as wide grow alternately on thin stalks that are about the same length as the leaves. Leaf surfaces are smooth, and the edges are untoothed.

FLOWERS/FRUIT: Funnel-shaped flowers that are typically 2 to 3 inches wide and deep grow singly or in small groups on **very long**, thin stemlets originating from leaf axils. The wide, outer edges are often purple, but may be pink, white or lavender. The center of the funnel is a contrasting color, and there are often 5 wide, somewhat blurry lines of another contrasting color running from the funnel's edge into the center. Fruits are egg-shaped capsules containing several dark seeds.

SEASON: Flowers are present from midsummer to early fall.

OTHER NAMES: Tall Morning Glory, Purple Morning Glory.

COMPARE: Leaves of Ivy-Leaved Morning Glory (*I. hederacea*; native annual) have **3 deep lobes** with slightly wavy edges. Flower stemlets are about ¼ inch long. Flowers are bluish-violet to pale pink, with a pale center; they open on sunny days and last one day. They are slightly more common in our area than escaped Common Morning Glory, and are found in roughly the same areas. • Bindweeds (pgs. 176 and 182) have funnel-shaped flowers, but the leaves are **arrowhead-shaped**.

Common Morning Glory, variable colors

Common Morning Glory

Ivy-Leaved Morning Glory

GETTING RID OF IT!

Morning Glory vines reproduce by seed, and can be prolific seed producers. Young vines are fairly easy to pull, but you'll have to keep at it for several years because seeds in the soil, even those buried fairly deeply, will continue to produce new plants for years.

WHAT'S IT GOOD FOR?

Hummingbirds are attracted to the flowers—and so are many people, accounting for the spread of this popular garden specimen.

Annual Bluegrass

(Poa annua)

OVERVIEW: The main problem with this non-native annual is that the entire plant dies in the heat of midsummer, leaving brown areas wherever it has become established in a lawn. It grows in clumps that are 3 to 12 inches high; stems are **round**. Leaf nodes that touch the ground form new roots, helping it to spread.

WHERE YOU'LL FIND IT: Sunny areas with rich, moist soil. It is most noticeable in lawns and on golf courses, but it also grows in pastures, landscaped areas, gardens, orchards and along roads. It is scattered throughout our region but is most common in the eastern half.

LEAVES: Yellowish-green leaves are up to 5½ inches long and very narrow. They are soft, hairless, and flat except at the tip, which is **pointed and slightly cupped**, resembling a canoe. Leaf sheaths are open, loose, smooth and flattened.

SEEDHEADS: Small clusters of short, branched stalks grow alternately on long stemlets arising from leaf axils; the entire seedhead is up to 3 inches long and one-third as wide. The spikelets* are loosely spreading, with bright green bases and white flowers; reddish tints are also present throughout. Seeds mature and disperse very quickly.

SEASON: In our region, Annual Bluegrass flowers in early spring and again in early fall. Seeds germinate and produce new plants in spring, then again in late summer through fall.

OTHER NAMES: Annual Meadow Grass, Six-Weeks Grass, Spear Grass.

COMPARE: Canada Bluegrass (*P. compressa*) is a non-native perennial that produces spreading rhizomes; it grows **singly or in small tufts**. Stems are **flattened** and up to **2 feet** tall. Leaves are similar to Annual Bluegrass, including the canoe-shaped tip. The seedhead is up to **4 inches** long. Canada Bluegrass is found in disturbed areas, seldom growing in lawns. It is quite common throughout our area except the Dakotas, where it is sparse or underreported.

*A spikelet is the floral unit of a grass plant; it contains both flower and seed.

Leaf tip (right)

GETTING RID OF IT!

Annual Bluegrass is tough to control because it grows during cool weather, when other lawn grasses are dormant or dying off, offering less competition. It also produces abundant seeds, which remain viable for years. Preemergent herbicides should be applied very early in fall, and again in early spring, right before the Bluegrass appears. Don't apply fertilizer during times that Bluegrass is actively growing. Keep mowing heights high; water deeply but infrequently to encourage growth of desirable grasses that may, over time, outcompete the Bluegrass.

WHAT'S IT GOOD FOR?

It can be used as livestock fodder and to make hay.

Quackgrass

(Elymus repens)

OVERVIEW: This non-native perennial grows in clumps and has extensive, creeping rhizomes, so it can create a dense colony. Stems are typically 2 to 3 feet long. They usually stand upright, but longer stems may slouch to the side.

WHERE YOU'LL FIND IT: Found in a variety of soil types, Quackgrass prefers moderate moisture levels and dies back in long, hot summers. It is found in disturbed areas including railroad embankments, pastures and roadsides; it also grows along the edges of lawns, gardens and landscaped areas. It is common throughout our region except the southern parts of Illinois and Indiana, and is listed as a noxious weed in Iowa.

LEAVES: **Rough-textured**, blue-green leaves grow alternately; they are 3 to 7 inches long and about ¼ inch wide. Leaves are flat, but tend to **twist or curl** over their length. The sheath at the leaf base is **open**, and has a pair of **sharply pointed ear-like projections** (called auricles) at the top.

SEEDHEADS: The seedhead is an **upright spike** up to 9 inches long that grows at the top of the stem; it resembles wheat. It is tightly packed with flattened, oblong spikelets* that grow at an **upward angle**. The spikelets are dusty green at first, maturing to light yellowish-brown.

SEASON: Quackgrass germinates in early spring. Seedheads are present from mid-spring to late summer.

OTHER NAMES: Couch Grass, Quick Grass, Witchgrass, *Elytrigia repens, Agropyron repens.*

COMPARE: Canada Wild Rye (*Elymus canadensis*; native perennial) is similar, but its auricles are **blunt**. The seedhead is a spike, but it **droops down**, and spikelets have long, **stiff bristles**. It grows in all states of our area but is uncommon to absent in the southern parts of Indiana and Ohio. • Smooth Brome (*Bromus inermis*; non-native perennial) looks similar before flowering, but its leaf sheaths **lack auricles**. The seedhead is a **loose, branched cluster**. It is found throughout our area.

*A spikelet is the floral unit of a grass plant; it contains both flower and seed.

GETTING RID OF IT!

For small outbreaks, pour boiling water over the plants, then pull plants when they die back; repeat as needed. Frequent mowing throughout the growing season can be effective in reducing large stands. Rhizome fragments produce new plants, so digging or tilling are not recommended. Some populations of Quackgrass are resistant to certain herbicides.

WHAT'S IT GOOD FOR?

Quackgrass is used for livestock forage, and also for hay; it is sometimes planted to control erosion. It provides good cover for small mammals, upland game birds and waterfowl. The rhizomes can reportedly be dried and ground to produce a flour substitute.

Foxtail

(Setaria spp.)

OVERVIEW: Two types of non-native annual Foxtail are common through-out our region. Both grow in tufts. Stems stand upright; each stem has 3 to 5 leaf nodes. Leaves are **flat** and grow alternately along the stem.

WHERE YOU'LL FIND IT: Full to partial sun, with medium to slightly low moisture levels. Foxtail is common in lawns, boulevards, pavement cracks and vacant lots; also grows in pastures, disturbed areas, and along roads and railroads. Green Foxtail (*S. viridis*) is common in all states of our region. Yellow Foxtail (*S. pumila*) is also found in all states of our region, but is uncommon to absent in western South Dakota and much of Ohio.

LEAVES: Green Foxtail leaves are up to 9 inches long and ½ inch wide, with a narrower base; plants are up to 2 feet tall. Leaves are **hairless** overall. • Leaves of Yellow Foxtail are similar to those of Green Foxtail, except there is a scattering of **long silky hairs** at the base of each leaf, above the sheath. Plants are up to **3 feet** tall.

SEEDHEADS: A single seedhead sits at the top of each stem. It is a long spike with tightly packed spikelets*, each with long bristles pointing outward from the spikelet; the seedhead is said to resemble the **bushy tail of a fox**. Green Foxtail spikes are up to 4 inches long; each spikelet has **1 to 3 greenish bristles**. Yellow Foxtail spikes are up to **5 inches** long; each spikelet has **5 to 20 yellow to yellowish-brown bristles**.

SEASON: Plants typically appear in spring; flowering occurs from late spring to early fall.

OTHER NAMES: Green Foxtail is also called Bottle Grass or Wild Millet. Yellow Foxtail is also called Pigeon Grass or Yellow Bristle Grass.

COMPARE: Giant Foxtail (*S. faberi*) is typically up to **4 feet tall**, although some sources report taller. Seedheads are up to **6 inches long**; each spikelet has **3 to 6 yellowish-green bristles**, and the seedheads tend to **nod**. In our area, it is found primarily in the southeastern two-thirds.

*A spikelet is the floral unit of a grass plant; it contains both flower and seed.

Green Foxtail

Green Foxtail

Yellow Foxtail
(above and right)

GETTING RID OF IT!

Foxtail plants appear in spring, and begin producing seedheads quickly. Pull young shoots as soon as they appear (they'll be lighter in color than most lawn grasses) and before they have a chance to spread; once the plants get bigger, a dandelion digger may be helpful to get long roots. Low mowing is hard on desirable grasses and will allow Foxtail to spread; mow at a height of 2½ to 3 inches. Aerate lawns every 2 years to promote healthy growth of desirable grasses.

WHAT'S IT GOOD FOR?

Foxtail Millet (*S. italica*) is grown for grain and used as hay for livestock, but these uses don't seem to be common for the Foxtails noted here.

Crabgrass

(Digitaria spp.)

OVERVIEW: Two types of non-native annual Crabgrass are common throughout our region. Both grow in tufts. The stems often sprawl outward, but may also stand upright, reaching heights of up to 2 feet. Leaves are flat and grow alternately along the stem from swollen nodes.

WHERE YOU'LL FIND IT: Full to partial sun, with medium moisture levels. Crabgrass is common in lawns, gardens, boulevards, pavement cracks and vacant lots; it also grows in meadows and along roads and railroads. Large Crabgrass (*D. sanguinalis*) is common in all states of our region except most of the Dakotas and the northern parts of Minnesota and Wisconsin. Smooth Crabgrass (*D. ischaemum*) is in the same areas as Large Crabgrass but less common; it also grows in the northern areas.

LEAVES: Large Crabgrass leaves are up to **6 inches** long and ¼ inch wide. **Fine white hairs** are scattered on both sides; hairs at the leaf base are typically longer and more noticeable. The sheath at the base of each leaf is **tightly rolled** and **hairy**. • Smooth Crabgrass **lacks the hairs** on the leaves and sheath. Leaves are typically 5 inches or shorter.

SEEDHEADS: **Loose sprays** of thin stalks **fan out like fingers** from the top of the stem; the tiny egg-shaped spikelets* are **pressed tightly** against the stalks. Large Crabgrass has several to as many as 15 stalks that are up to 7 inches long; Smooth Crabgrass has 6 or fewer stalks, and they are 4 inches long or less. Each plant can produce thousands of seeds.

SEASON: Plants typically appear from mid-spring into summer. Large Crabgrass flowers from summer through early fall; Smooth Crabgrass may flower through mid-fall or even later.

OTHER NAMES: Large Crabgrass is also called Common Crabgrass or Hairy Crabgrass. Smooth Crabgrass is also called Small Crabgrass.

COMPARE: Bermudagrass (*Cynodon dactylon*; non-native) has similar seedheads, but its leaves are **finer** and somewhat **wiry**; it spreads by **stolons** (runners). In our area it is found in the southeastern one-third.

*A spikelet is the floral unit of a grass plant; it contains both flower and seed.

Large Crabgrass (all 4)

GETTING RID OF IT!

Crabgrass sprouts at a soil temperature of 55°F. Apply a preemergent herbicide in spring, when the soil is about 53°F. Pull young shoots as soon as they appear; they'll be lighter in color than lawn grasses, and easy to pull. Crabgrass roots at the nodes, and if you want to try pulling it once it's begun to spread, you'll need to follow the stems to get all the roots—and you may pull out desirable grasses at the same time. Mow at a height of 2½ to 3 inches to discourage Crabgrass. Boiling water may be effective on Crabgrass growing in pavement cracks.

WHAT'S IT GOOD FOR?

Livestock will eat Crabgrass. The seeds can be ground to use like flour.

Yellow Nutsedge

(Cyperus esculentus)

OVERVIEW: Unlike true grasses that have round, hollow stems between leaf nodes, sedges have stems that are **triangular in cross section**. Yellow Nutsedge is a non-native perennial with an unbranched central stem up to 2½ feet tall; the stem is triangular and hairless. Many leaves grow around the base of the stem. Floral spikes grow at the top of the stem, on thin stemlets that **originate from a central point** (umbellate).

WHERE YOU'LL FIND IT: Sunny to lightly shaded areas with moist to wet soil. It is most common in cultivated fields, pastures and wetlands, but is also found in gardens, ditches and damp turf areas such as low spots in golf courses, parks and lawns. It is quite common in Iowa and Illinois, and scattered to locally common in the remaining states of our area.

LEAVES: The smooth, stiff, light-green leaves are up to 18 inches long and ⅓ inch wide; they may appear waxy. The midvein is **deeply creased** and leaf tips are **sharply pointed**. Leaf sheaths are pale and closed.

SEEDHEADS: One to 3 floral spikes, each 1 to 3 inches long, grow on each thin stemlet at the top of the plant (see Overview). **Several leaflike bracts grow in a whorl at the base of the floral array**. **Golden-brown to yellow** linear spikelets* up to ¾ inch long grow perpendicular to the spike in groups of 4. The seeds are brown and football-shaped.

SEASON: Young plants begin to appear in mid to late spring. Blooming takes place from midsummer to early fall.

OTHER NAMES: Chufa, Field Nutsedge, Nut-Grass, Watergrass.

COMPARE: The native Straw-Colored Flatsedge (*C. strigosus*; perennial) appears very similar to Yellow Nutsedge, but its spikelets are **green to yellowish-green**, and there are up to **8 bracts** under each floral cluster. In our region it is found primarily in the eastern two-thirds, although it is uncommon or absent from the northern parts of Minnesota, Wisconsin and Michigan. It does not grow in North Dakota.

*A spikelet is the floral unit of a grass plant; it contains both flower and seed.

GETTING RID OF IT!

Yellow Nutsedge has an extensive, complicated root system consisting of roots, bulbs, rhizomes, and tubers (see pg. 9 for a photo). It reproduces via tubers and rhizomes and can form large colonies; the tubers overwinter and produce new plants in spring. The best method for removal is to dig out the dirt 6 to 12 inches down to ensure you get the entire root system, then dispose of it; don't try composting, as the tubers will probably survive. Herbicides are available that specifically target Nutsedges.

WHAT'S IT GOOD FOR?

The tubers of Yellow Nutsedge are used to make an almond-flavored drink. Waterfowl eat the tubers and spikelets of both Sedges listed here.

Goosegrass

(Eleusine indica)

OVERVIEW: Goosegrass is a non-native annual that thrives in areas with compacted soil. It grows in a **wide-spreading** tuft with multiple stems radiating out from the crown. Stems may be nearly 3 feet long and may stand upright, although they more commonly sprawl to the sides; the plant may appear nearly flat, looking as though it's been walked on (which it probably has). It may be dense and bushy-looking, or thin and scraggly. The crown sometimes appears to be sunken into the soil.

WHERE YOU'LL FIND IT: Hot, sunny areas, with fairly dry soil to moderate soil moisture; Goosegrass can survive periods of drought. It tolerates foot traffic and is found near athletic fields, along paths and driveways, and in disturbed areas such as vacant lots; it may appear in lawns and also grows in croplands, pastures and along roads. It is primarily a species of the southeastern U.S.; in our region, it is fairly common throughout the southern half.

LEAVES: The smooth, dull green leaves are 2 to 13 inches long and about ¼ inch wide; they are **folded along the midvein**. The sheaths at the base are **flattened** and **white** to silver; some say this makes the plant resemble a wagon wheel when viewed from the top.

SEEDHEADS: A **loose spray** of thin stalks **fans out like fingers** from the top of the stem; the tiny, flattened spikelets[*] are **pressed tightly** against the stalks. Plants typically have 2 to 6 stalks (sometimes more), each 1½ to 6 inches long, growing in a **whorl** from a central point; a single stalk frequently grows below the rest.

SEASON: Goosegrass germinates several weeks later than Crabgrass (pg. 196). The seedheads are present from midsummer into mid-fall.

OTHER NAMES: Wiregrass, Silver Crabgrass, Crowfoot Grass.

COMPARE: Smooth Crabgrass (pg. 196) appears similar, but Goosegrass can be identified by the **flattened, whitish sheaths** at the center of the plant. Also, Crabgrass leaves are **flat**, not folded.

[*]A spikelet is the floral unit of a grass plant; it contains both flower and seed.

Seedhead (right)

GETTING RID OF IT!

Goosegrass appears at a soil temperature of 60°F–65°F. Apply a pre-emergent herbicide when the soil is about 58°F. Pull Goosegrass shoots when they first appear; look for the distinctive white center. Goosegrass thrives in compacted areas, so the first step in preventing repeat occurrences is soil aeration, along with soil amendments to increase fertility. Increased mowing height will also cool the soil and allow less sunlight to penetrate into the shallow depths where Goosegrass thrives.

WHAT'S IT GOOD FOR?

Goosegrass is a poverty food in the Tropics, where it originated. Young seedlings are edible raw or cooked. Seeds can be cooked like millet.

Barnyardgrass

(Echinochloa crus-galli)

OVERVIEW: This non-native is a summer annual. Upright stems are un-branched, and may grow **solitary**. Young plants often sprawl sideways, and the sprawling stems may branch, with each branch sending up an unbranched stem; this creates a small tuft of upright stems. Stems are round and smooth, and can be up to 5 feet tall.

WHERE YOU'LL FIND IT: Full sun to part shade, with adequate moisture. It is found in weedy urban boulevards and vacant lots, along roads and railroads, around ponds and swamps, and in fields, pastures, waste dumps and moist ditches. It is fairly common throughout much our area, but is scattered to absent in much of the Dakotas, the southern two-thirds of Illinois, and the northern parts of Wisconsin and Michigan.

LEAVES: The smooth, bluish-green leaves grow alternately. They are typically 4 to 8 inches long and ½ inch wide at the base, with a pointed tip. Leaves have a **prominent, pale midrib** which is slightly depressed (particularly at the sheath), making the leaf appear **creased**. The sheath at the leaf base is open and smooth, and may be tinged with red. Leaf bases at the center of the plant may be reddish.

SEEDHEADS: Short stemlets covered with clusters of densely packed spikelets* grow at intervals along the flowering stalk and also at the top; the flowering stalk is up to 10 inches long and may nod slightly. Spikelets are **greenish to purplish**, and are shaped like a **pointed oval** about ⅛ inch long; some have thin bristles at the pointed end, but these are sometimes absent.

SEASON: Barnyardgrass germinates in late spring to early summer, and blooms from midsummer to early fall.

OTHER NAMES: Billion-Dollar Grass, Japanese Millet, Barn-Grass.

COMPARE: Junglerice (*E. colona*; non-native) has similar seedheads, but its leaves have **purple bands**. It is found in wet habitat in the southern U.S. and grows in a few counties each in Illinois, Ohio and Wisconsin.

*A spikelet is the floral unit of a grass plant; it contains both flower and seed.

GETTING RID OF IT!

Barnyardgrass spreads by seeds, and can form colonies. It has a shallow root system and is fairly easy to pull up. Be sure to get it before the plants go to seed. Mulch will prevent seeds from germinating.

WHAT'S IT GOOD FOR?

Songbirds and waterfowl eat the seeds, and plants in wet areas offer cover to waterfowl. The leafy stems can be used as livestock feed while still green, but the plants are not suitable for hay. Barnyardgrass has been used to leach salt and heavy metals from contaminated ground, and has also been used medicinally to relieve sores, hemorrhages and other complaints. Seeds can be used as a grain for human consumption.

Stinkgrass

(Eragrostis cilianensis)

OVERVIEW: This non-native annual is a warm-season grass that grows in **open tufts**. Stems are narrow, hairless and up to 2 feet long; they often sprawl sideways. Stinkgrass has a **foul smell**, especially when crushed.

WHERE YOU'LL FIND IT: Stinkgrass prefers full sun and is often found in open areas such as roadsides, vacant lots, pastures, gardens, patchy lawns and along railroad tracks. It can grow in poor soil, and is drought tolerant. Found throughout our region, although it is less common in western Ohio and the northern parts of Wisconsin and Michigan.

LEAVES: The flat, faintly ribbed leaves are up to 6 inches long and ¼ inch wide. **Clear, dot-like glands** appear on the edges and around the base of the sheath, which has **thin, fine hairs** along its upper margin; the dot-like glands are the source of the foul odor.

SEEDHEADS: Small clusters of short, branched stalks grow alternately on long stemlets arising from leaf axils; the entire seedhead is up to 7½ inches long. **Silvery-green** spikelets* up to ½ inch long are bunched along the branched stalks. The spikelets are flattened and elongated, with a rounded base; they have a **sheaf-like** pattern, created by **up to 40** individual, **overlapping florets**. Florets are replaced by dark grains.

SEASON: Stinkgrass germinates in early summer, and blooms from midsummer into early fall.

OTHER NAMES: Gray Lovegrass, Skunkgrass, Candy Grass.

COMPARE: Two related native grasses with similarly shaped spikelets are nearly as common in our area, although they are less reported in the Dakotas. Both **lack the dot-like glands**. • Tufted Lovegrass (*E. pectinacea*; annual) grows as a sprawling, **moderately dense tuft** up to 2 feet high; it also grows in short clumps from sidewalk cracks. Spikelets are about **half the size** of those on Stinkgrass, and have **15 or fewer** florets. • Seedheads of Purple Lovegrass (*E. spectabilis*; perennial) are **purplish** and **very wispy**, with a **single purple spikelet** on each stalk.

*A spikelet is the floral unit of a grass plant; it contains both flower and seed.

GETTING RID OF IT!

Stinkgrass is fairly easy to pull; keep an eye out for newly sprouted plants throughout the growing season. Always pull plants before the seedheads ripen and produce the dark grains, which will sprout and produce new plants. Regular mowing will also prevent the plants from reseeding. Stinkgrass rarely competes in areas with abundant, healthy vegetation, so the best method of long-term control is to increase the vigor of desirable plants. Mulching will also help prevent the spread of Stinkgrass.

WHAT'S IT GOOD FOR?

Apparently, not much. It is toxic to horses, and livestock don't browse it due to its smell. It is not effective at erosion control.

RECOMMENDED REFERENCES

The following websites present reliable information and photos or illustrations that may be of interest to readers. Some make heavy use of scientific terms; if you're unsure about what something means, search online for a definition.

Common Plants of Wisconsin, University of Wisconsin—Stevens Point. (www4.uwsp.edu/biology/courses/plantid/cp-hires-main.htm)

Gary A. Fewless Herbarium at the Cofrin Center for Biodiversity, University of Wisconsin—Green Bay. (uwgb.edu/biodiversity/herbarium/)

Illinois Wildflowers Info, Dr. John Hilty. (illinoiswildflowers.info)

Michigan State University Turf Weeds, Ronald Calhoun. (msuturfweeds.net)

Minnesota Wildflowers, Katy Chayka and Peter M. Dziuk. (minnesotawildflowers.info)

Missouri Plants, Dan Tenaglia. (missouriplants.com/index.html)

The National Gardening Association, Weed Library. (garden.org/learn/library/weeds/)

Ohio Perennial and Biennial Weed Guide, The Ohio State University. (oardc.ohio-state.edu/weedguide/)

Weed ID Guide at the Division of Plant Sciences, University of Missouri. (weedid.missouri.edu/)

Weed Science at the University of Illinois. (weeds.cropsci.illinois.edu/weedid.htm)

Weedy and Invasive Grasses Found in Iowa at Grasses of Iowa, Iowa State University. (www.eeob.iastate.edu/research/IowaGrasses/weedy.html)

Additional References Used by the Author

Biota of North America Program. (bonap.org)

Bryson, Charles T. and DeFelice, Michael S. *Weeds of the Midwestern United States & Central Canada*. Athens, GA: University of Georgia Press, 2010.

Del Tredici, Peter. *Wild Urban Plants of the Northeast*. Ithaca, NY: Comstock Publishing Associates, Cornell University Press, 2010.

Dickinson, Richard and Royer, Frances. *Weeds of North America*. Chicago: The University of Chicago Press, 2014.

Early Detection & Distribution Mapping Systems (https://www.eddmaps.org/)

Gift, Nancy. *Good Weed, Bad Weed*. Pittsburgh, PA; St. Lynn's Press, 2011.

Tekiela, Stan. *Wildflowers of Wisconsin* (also other states in the region). Cambridge, MN: Adventure Publications, 2000.

Thayer, Samuel. *The Forager's Harvest*. Ogema, WI: Forager's Harvest, 2006.

Turf Tips, Purdue Extension. (purdueturftips.blogspot.com/)

INDEX

Note: **Bold text** indicates species description. Alternate names are in parentheses.

A

Acalypha rhomboidea, virginica, **102–103**

Achillea millefolium, **88–89**

Ageratina altissima, **104–105**

Agropyron repens, 192

Alliaria petiolata (officinalis), **70–71**

Alsike Clover, 16, **32–33**

Alternate leaf arrangement, definition and example, 13

Alyssum, Hoary, **82–83**

Amaranth (several), **66**

Amaranthus hybridus, retroflexus, spinosus, **66–67**

Ambrosia artemisiifolia, psilostachya, **56–57**

Ambrosia trifida, **58–59**

Amendments, 21

American Bellflower, **172**

American Germander, **166**

Annual Bluegrass, **190–191**

Annual Meadow Grass, 190

Annual plants, definition, 8

Annual Ragweed, 56

Annual Sowthistle, 136

Anthemis cotula, **90–91**

Anther, definition and examples, 14–15

Arctium lappa, minus, **162–163**

Arrowhead-shaped leaves, definition and example, 11

Asclepias exaltata, syriaca, **158–159**

Asiatic Dayflower, **50–51**

Atropa belladonna, 187

Aunt Lucy, **24–25**

Avens (several), **74–75**

B

Baby's Breath, False, **76**

Balkan Catchfly, **86–87**

Balsam Apple, Wild, 184

Bamboo, Japanese, 106

Banner petal, definition, 16

Barbarea genus, 108

Barbarea vulgaris, **108–109**

Barn-Grass, 202

Barnyardgrass, **202–203**

Basal cluster, definition, 8

Beads, weed seeds used as, 185

Bedstraw, Fragrant, **76–77**

Beer, weeds used to make, 89, 181

Beggar's Ticks, Tall (Big Devil's) and Common (Devil's), **144–145**

Bellflower, Creeping and American, **172–173**

Bermudagrass, **196**

Berteroa incana, **82–83**

Bidens frondosa, vulgata, **144–145**

Biennial plants, definition, 8

Big-Bract Verbena, **54–55**

Big Devil's Beggarticks, 144

Billion-Dollar Grass, 202

Bindweed, Black, **176–177**, 188

Bindweed, Hedge (Giant) and Field, **182–183**, 188

Biodiesel, weeds used to make, 69

Bipinnate leaves, definition and example, 12

Birdfoot Deervetch, 126

Birdsfoot Trefoil, 16, **126–127**

Bitter Buttons, 140

Bittersweet Nightshade, 94, **186–187**

Black Bindweed, **176–177**

Black Clover, 42

Black Medick (Black Medic), **42–43**, 120

Black Nightshade (Eastern Black Nightshade), **94–95**, 186

Black-Seeded Plantain, **22**

Black Thistle, 164

Bladder Campion, **86–87**

Bladder Hibiscus, 100

Bluebell, Creeping, 172

Blue Dayflower, 50

Bluegrass, Annual and Canada, **190–191**

Blue Violet, Common, **48–49**

Boneset, Common (Tall), **104**

Bottle Grass, 194

Bracts, definition and example, 15

Branched stalks, definition and example, 17

Branching cluster, definition and example, 17

Brassica genus, 108

Brassicaceae family, 108

Bristly Buttercup, **130–131**

Broad-Leaved Plantain, 22

Brome, Smooth, **192**

Bromus inermis, **192**

Buckwheat, Climbing False and Wild, **176–177**

Bull Thistle, **164–165**

Bur Cucumber, **184–185**

Burdock, Common (Lesser) and Great, **162–163**

Burn Weed, Burnweed, 64, 110

Butter-and-Eggs, 128

Buttercup
  Bristly, **130–131**
  Cursed, **112**
  Little-Leaf (Early Wood,
    Kidney-Leaf, Small-
    Flowered), **112–113**
  Tall (Common, Giant,
    Meadow), **130–131**
Buttonweed, 148

C

Calystegia sepium, **182–183**
Calyx, definition, 14
*Campanula rapunculoides,
  rotundifolia,* **172–173**
*Campanulastrum
  americanum,* 172
Campion, White (Evening)
  and Bladder, **86–87**
Canada Bluegrass, **190–191**
Canada Fleabane, 98
Canada Goldenrod, **142–143**
Canada Lettuce, 138
Canada Thistle,
  160–161, 168
Canada Violet, **48–49**
Canada Wild Rye, **192**
Candy Grass, 204
Capsella bursa-pastoris,
  80–81
Cardaria draba, 68
*Carduus acanthoides, nu-
  tans,* **164–165**
Carpel, definition, 14
Carpetweed, **30–31,** 46
Carrot, Wild, 96
Catchfly, Balkan, **86–87**
Cat Mint, 166
Catnip, **166–167**
Catweed, 166
*Centaurea maculosa, repens,
  stoebe, stoebe* ssp.
  micranthos, **168–169**
*Cerastium fontanum,
  vulgatum,* **26–27**
Chamaesyce genus, 28

*Chamerion
  angustifolium,* 170
Chamomile, Stinking, 90
Chamomile, Wild, 44
Cheeseweed,
  Cheeseplant, 148
Chenopodium album, **62–63**
Chickweed, 82
  Common, **26–27**
  Giant (Water), **26**
  Indian Chickweed, 30
  Mouse-Ear, **26–27**
  Whorled Chickweed, 30
Chigger Weed, 96
*Chrysanthemum
  leucanthemum,* 90
*Chrysanthemum
  vulgare,* 140
Chufa, 198
Climbing Nightshade, 186
Cinquefoil
  Common (Oldfield), **34–35**
  Rough (Norwegian),
    132–133
  Silver, **34–35**
  Sulfur, **132–133**
Cirsium arvense, discolor,
  160–161
Cirsium vulgare, **164–165**
Clasping leaf attachment,
  definition and example, 13
Cleavers, 30, **76–77**
Climbing False Buckwheat,
  176–177
Climbing Nightshade, 186
Clover, 16, 120
  Alsike, 16, **32–33**
  Black, 42
  Golden, **42–43,** 120
  Hop, 42, 120
  Lemon, 120
  Low Hop, **42–43**
  Red, **32-33**
  White (Dutch), 16, **32–33**
Cockle, White, 86
Coffee substitute, weeds as,
  37, 137
Commelina communis,
  50–51

Common Amaranth, 66
Common Beggar's Ticks,
  144–145
Common Blue Violet, **48–49**
Common Boneset, **104**
Common Burdock, **162–163**
Common Buttercup, 130
Common Chickweed, **26–27**
Common Cinquefoil, **34–35**
Common Crabgrass, 196
Common Daisy, 90
Common Dandelion, **36–37**
Common Dayflower, 50
Common Groundsel,
  110–111
Common Hops, **180–181**
Common Mallow, **148–149**
Common Melilot, 116
Common Milkweed,
  158–159
Common Morning Glory,
  182, **188–189**
Common Motherwort, 152
Common Mullein, **134–135**
Common Nettle, 64
Common Parsnip, 114
Common Peppergrass,
  72–73, 80
Common Plantain, **22–23**
Common Purslane, 28, 30,
  46–47
Common Quickweed, 92
Common Ragweed, **56–57**
Common Ragwort, 110
Common Sowthistle
  (Annual), **136–137**
Common St. John's
  Wort, 124
Common Vetch, **154**
Common Yarrow, 88
Composite flower, definition
  and examples, 14, 16
Compound leaves, definition
  and examples, 12
Conium maculatum, **96–97**

Convolvulus arvensis, sepium, **182**

Conyza canadensis, **98–99**

Copperleaf, Rhombic Copperleaf, Virginia Copperleaf, **102**

Cordate leaves, definition and example, 11

Corn Speedwell, **54–55**

Coronilla varia, 154

Corymb, definition and example, 17

Couch Grass, 192

Cow Parsnip, **78–79**, 96, 114

Crabgrass (several), **196–197**, 200

Creeping Bellflower, **172–173**

Creeping Bluebell, 172

Creeping Charlie, 52

Creeping Jenny, **40–41**

Creeping Yellow Loosestrife, 40

Cress, Hoary, **68**

Cress, Winter, 108

Crowfoot, Cursed, **112**

Crown Vetch, **154–155**

Cucumber, Wild and Bur, **184–185**

Curly Dock (Curled Dock), **122–123**

Cursed Crowfoot (Cursed Buttercup), **112**

Cyathium, cyathia, 118

Cyme, about, 17

Cynodon dactylon, **196**

Cyperus esculentus, strigosus, **198–199**

Cypress Spurge, **118**

D

Daisies, structure, 16

Daisy, Oxeye (Common), 16, **90–91**

Daisy, Peruvian, 92

Dalmatian Toadflax, **128**

Dandelion, Common, 16, **36–37**, 136

Dandelion, Red-Seeded, **36**

Daucus carota, **96–97**

Dayflower, Asiatic (Blue, Common), **50–51**

Deadly Nightshade, 187

Deeply lobed leaves, definition and example, 11

Deervetch, Birdfoot, 126

Descurainia genus, 108

Devil's Beggar Ticks, 144

Devil's Claw, 126

Devil's Grip, 30

Devil's Paintbrush, 146

Digging weeds, advice and techniques, 19–20

Digitaria ischaemum, sanguinalis, **196–197**

Dioecious, definition and example, 86–87

Disc Mayweed, 44

Disk flowers, about and examples, 14, 16

Dock, Curly (Curled, Yellow), **122–123**

Dock, Pale, **122**

Dog Fennel, 44, **90–91**, 140

Downy Yellow Violet, **48–49**

Duchesnea indica, 38

Dutch Clover, 32

Dwarf Mallow, **148–149**

Dye, weeds used for, 61, 125, 129

E

Early Wood Buttercup, 112

Eastern Black Nightshade, 94

Eastern Poison Ivy, 60, **174–175**

Echinochloa colona, crus-galli, **202–203**

Echinocystis lobata, **184–185**

Edible weeds, 6
  flowers, 49, 51, 71, 109, 121
  fruits, 39, 95, 121, 149
  leaves, 23, 27, 31, 37, 47, 49, 51, 53, 63, 65, 67, 69, 71, 73, 77, 81, 91, 99, 109, 121, 123, 137, 139, 149, 183
  roots and tubers, 37, 75, 97, 115, 163, 183, 193, 199
  seeds and seedpods, 63, 67, 73, 81, 201, 203
  stems, seedlings and shoots, 47, 69, 77, 79, 183, 201
  see also: Beer, Coffee substitute, Flour, Jelly, Tea, Wine; ***also see note about consuming wild plants on page 215***

Egg-shaped leaves, definition and example, 10

Eleusine indica, **200–201**

Elliptic or elliptical leaves, definition and example, 10

Ellisia nyctelea, **24–25**

Elymus canadensis, repens, **192–193**

Elytrigia repens, 192

English Plantain, **22**

Epilobium angustifolium, **170**

Eragrostis cilianensis, pectinacea, spectabilis, **204–205**

Erechtites hieraciifolius, **110–111**

Erigeron canadensis, 98

Erysimum genus, 108

Eupatorium perfoliatum, rugosum, **104**

Euphorbia cyparissias, **118**

Euphorbia esula (virgata), **118–119**

Euphorbia glyptosperma, humistrata, maculata, **28–29**

Evening Campion, 86

Evening Lychnis, 86

F

Fallopia convolvulus, scandens, **176–177**

Fallopia japonica, 106

False Baby's Breath, **76**

False Buckwheat, Climbing, **176–177**

Fanweed, 68

Fat Hen, 62

Fennel, Dog, 44, **90–91**, 140

Field Bindweed, **182–183**

Field Hawkweed, 146

Field Nutsedge, 198

Field Pennycress, **68–69**

Field Peppergrass, **72**

Field Thistle, **160–161**
as alternate name for Canada Thistle, 160

Filament, definition and examples, 14–15

Fireweed, **170**

Five-Leaved Ivy, **178–179**

Flaming weeds, about, 20

Flannel Plant, 134

Flatsedge, Straw-Colored, **198**

Fleabane, Canada, 98

Fleece Flower, Japanese, 106

Florets, definition and examples, 16

Flour, substitute from weed rhizomes, 193, 197

Flower-of-an-Hour, 100

Flowers, about, 14
arrangement on stem, 17
illustration of flower parts, 15

Four o'Clock, Wild (Heart-leaf) and Hairy (White), **156–157**

Foxtail, Giant, Green and Yellow, **194–195**

Foxtail Millet, 195

Fragaria virginiana, vesca, **38**

Fragrant Bedstraw, **76–77**

Frenchweed, 68

Fruits, about and examples, 14–15

G

Galinsoga, Hairy and Small-Flowered, **92–93**

Galinsoga parviflora, quadriradiata, **92–93**

Galium aparine, mollugo, triflorum, **76–77**

Garlic, Hedge, 70

Garlic Mustard, **70–71**

Germander, American, **166**

Geum aleppicum, canadense, laciniatum, **74–75**

Giant Bindweed, 182

Giant Buttercup, 130

Giant Chickweed, **26**

Giant Foxtail, **194**

Giant Goldenrod, **142**

Giant Hogweed, **78–79**

Giant Knotweed, **106**

Giant Ragweed, **58–59**

Gill-over-the-Ground, 52

Glechoma hederacea, **52–53**

Golden Buttons, 140

Golden Clover, **42–43**, 120

Goldenrod, 98, **142–143**

Goosefoot, 62

Goosegrass, **200–201**

Grapes, Wild, **178**

Gray Lovegrass, 204

Great Burdock, **162**

Great Mullein, 134

Great Nettle, 64

Great Ragweed, 58

Green-Flowered Peppergrass, **72**

Green Foxtail, **194–195**

Green Pigweed, 66

Green Purslane, 46

Ground Ivy, **52–53**, 70, 148, 149

Groundsel, Common, **110–111**

H

Hairy Crabgrass, 196

Hairy Four o'Clock, **156**

Hairy Galinsoga, **92–93**

Hastate leaves, definition and example, 11

Hawkweed, Meadow (Field), 36, **146–147**

Hawkweed, Orange, **146–147**

Hay Fever Weed, 56

Hayfever, 56, 58, 143

Heartleaf Four o'Clock, 156

Heart-shaped leaves, definition and example, 11

Hedge Bindweed, **182–183**

Hedge Garlic, 70

Hemlock, Poison, **96–97**

Henbit, **52**

Heracleum lanatum, mantegazzianum, maximum, **78–79**

Herbicides, about, 20–21

Hibiscus, Bladder, 100

Hibiscus trionum, **100–101**

Hieracium aurantiacum, caespitosum, **146–147**

Hoary Alyssum, **82–83**

Hoary Cress, **68**

Hoary False Madwort, 82

Hogweed, 78
Giant, **78–79**
Little, 46

Honey and honeybees, 43, 59, 117, 143, 169

Hop Clover, 42, 120

Hops, Japanese and Common, **180–181**

Horse Nettle and Carolina Horse Nettle, **84–85**, 94

Horseweed, 6, 7, **98–99**

Humulus japonicus, lupulus, scandens, **180–181**

Hypericum perforatum, punctatum, **124–125**

I

Indian Chickweed, 30

Indian Strawberry, 38

Insect repellent, weeds as, 141, 167

Introduced plants, definition, 6

Invasive plants, definition, 7

Ipomoea hederacea, purpurea, **188–189**

Itch Weed, 64

Ivy, Five-Leaved, **178–179**

Ivy-Leaved Morning Glory, **188–189**

J

Japanese Bamboo, 106

Japanese Fleece Flower, 106

Japanese Hops, **180–181**

Japanese Knotweed, **106–107**

Japanese Millet, 202

Jelly, weeds used to make, 97

Jenny, Creeping, **40–41**

Junglerice, **202**

K

Keel petals, definition, 16

Kidney-Leaf Buttercup, 112

Kidney-shaped leaves, definition and example, 11

King Devil, 146

Klamath Weed, 124

Knapweed, Russian and Spotted, **168–169**

Knotweed, Giant and Japanese, **106–107**

Knotweed, Prostrate, **28–29**, 46, 47

L

Lactuca canadensis, scariola, serriola, **138–139**

Lady's Thumb, **150–151**

Lambsquarters (Lamb's-Quarters), **62–63**

Lamium amplexicaule, **52**

Lance-like or lanceolate leaves, definition and example, 11

Laportea canadensis, **64**

Large Crabgrass, **196**

Late Goldenrod, 142

Leaf arrangement and attachment, examples, 13

Leaf shapes, examples, 10–11

Leafy Spurge, 98, **118–119**

Lemon Clover, 120

Leonurus cardiaca, **152–153**

*Lepidium
    campestre,* **72**
    densiflorum, **72**
    draba, **68**
    virginicum, **72–73**

Lesser Burdock, 162

Lettuce, Prickly (Opium) and Wild (Canada), 36, 136, **138–139**

Leucanthemum vulgare, **90–91**

Linaria dalmatica, vulgaris, **128–129**

Lincoln, Abraham and Nancy, 104, 105

Linear leaves, definition and example, 11

Lion's Ear, Lion's Tail, 152

Little Hogweed, 46

Little-Leaf Buttercup, **112–113**

Loosestrife, Creeping Yellow, 40

Loosestrife, Purple (Spiked), 5, **170–171**

Lotus corniculatus, **126–127**

Lovegrass, Gray, 204
    Purple and Tufted, **204**

Low-Growing Spurges (several), **28–29**, 30, 46

Low Hop Clover, **42–43**

Lysimachia nummularia, **40–41**

Lythrum palustre, salicaria, **170–171**

M

Madwort, Hoary False, 82

Mallow, Common and Dwarf (Round-Leaved), **148–149**

Mallow, Venice, **100–101**

Malva neglecta, pusilla, rotundifolia, **148–149**

Matricaria discoidea, matricarioides, perforata, **44–45**

Mayweed, Disc, 44

Mayweed, Scentless False, 44

Meadow Buttercup, 130

Meadow Grass, Annual, 190

Meadow Hawkweed, 36, **146–147**

Medicago lupulina, **42–43**

Medicinal purposes, weeds used for, 23, 29, 35, 39, 45, 55, 61, 69, 89, 103, 107, 109, 123, 125, 131, 133, 135, 137, 139, 141, 143, 153, 157, 163, 167, 185, 203

Medick (or Medic), Black, **42–43**, 120

Melilot, Common, Yellow, 116

Melilotus alba, officinalis, officinalis alba, **116–117**

Mentha arvensis, **152–153**

Mercury, Three-Seeded (Rhomboid), 102

Milkweed, Common (Showy) and Poke, **158–159**

Millet, Foxtail, 195

Millet, Japanese, 202

Millet, Wild, 194

Mint, Wild, **152–153**

Mirabilis albida, nyctaginea, **156–157**

Mock Strawberry, **38–39**

Mollugo verticillata, **30–31**

Monarch butterflies, 159

Moneywort, 40

Morning Glory, Common (Tall, Purple), 182, **188–189**

Morning Glory, Ivy-Leaved, **188–189**

Morning Glory, Wild, 182

Motherwort, **152–153**

Mouse-Ear Chickweed, **26–27**

Mouse Flower, 50

Mowing weeds, advice and techniques, 19

Mulching, about, 21

Mullein, Common (Great), **134-135**

Mustard family, 108

Mustard, Garlic, **70–71**

Myosoton aquaticum, **26**

N

Native plants, definition, 6

Nepeta cataria, **166–167**

Nettle, Horse, **84–85**, 94

Nettle, Stinging (Common, Great), **64–65**, 102

Nettle, Wood, **64**

Nightshade, Bittersweet (Climbing), 94, **186–187**

Nightshade, Black (Eastern Black, West Indian), **94–95**, 186

Nightshade, Deadly, 187

Nodding Smartweed, **150–151**

Nodding Thistle, **164–165**

Non-native plants, definition, 6

Norwegian Cinquefoil, 132

Noxious plants, definition, 7

Nut-Grass, 198

Nutsedge, Yellow (Field), **198–199**

O

Oblong leaves, definition and example, 11

Obovate leaves, definition and example, 10

Ocrea, 28, 122, 150, 151, 176

Oldfield Cinquefoil, 34

Old-Field Five-Fingers, 34

Old-Man-in-the-Spring, 110

Opium Lettuce, 138

Opposite leaf arrangement, definition and example, 13

Orange Hawkweed, **146–147**

Orbicular leaves, definition and example, 11

Ovary, 14

Ovate leaves, definition and example, 10

Overseeding, about, 21

Oxalis stricta, **120–121**

Oxeye Daisy, 16, **90–91**

P

Pale Dock, **122**

Pale Smartweed, 150

Palmate leaves, definition and example, 12

Panais Sauvage, 114

Panicle, about, 17

Parietaria pensylvanica, **102**

Parsnip, Cow, **78–79**, 96, 114

Parsnip, Wild (Common), 78, 79, **114–115**

Parthenocissus inserta, quinquefolia, vitacea, **178–179**

Pastinaca sativa, **114–115**

Pea-like flowers, definition and examples, 16

Pellitory, Pennsylvania, **102**

Pennsylvania Pellitory, **102**

Pennsylvania Smartweed, **150**

Pennycress, Field, **68–69**

Peppergrass (several), 6, **72–73**, 80

Pepperweed, Virginia, 72

Perennial plants, definition, 8

Perennial Sowthistle, **136–137**

Persicaria lapathifolia, maculosa, pensylvanica, **150–151**

Peruvian Daisy, 92

Petal, definition and example, 14–15
types (banner, keel, wing), 16

Petiole, definition and example, 13

Phytophotodermatitis, 78, 114

Pigeon Grass, 194

Pigweed
as name for Lambsquarters, 62
Green, 66
Rough, 62, **66–67**
Smooth, 66

Pilewort, 98, **110–111**

Pineappleweed, **44–45**

Pinnate leaves, definition and example, 12

Pistil, definition, 14

Plantago lanceolata, major, rugelii, **22–23**

Plantain (several), **22-23**

Plumajillo, 88

Plumeless Thistle, **164–165**

Poa annua, compressa, **190–191**

Poison Hemlock, **96–97**

Poison Ivy, 6
Eastern, 60, **174–175**
Western, **60–61**, 174

Poison Vine, 174

Poke Milkweed, **158**

Pollan, Michael, 63

Pollination, about, 14

Polygonum
aviculare, **28**
convolvulus, 176
cuspidatum, 106
persicaria, 150

Portulaca oleracea, **46–47**

Potentilla argentea, simplex,
34–35

Potentilla indica, **38–39**

Potentilla norvegica, recta,
132–133

Preventing weed growth, 21

Prickly Lettuce (Opium
Lettuce), 36, 136, **138–139**

Prickly Sowthistle, 136

Prostrate Knotweed, **28–29**,
46, 47

Prostrate Vervain, 54

Pulling weeds, advice and
techniques, 18–19

Purple Loosestrife, 5,
170–171

Purple Lovegrass, **204**

Purple Morning Glory, 188

Purslane, Common, 28, 30,
46–47

Purslane, Green, 46

Pursley, 46

Q

Quackgrass, **192–193**

Queen Anne's Lace, 78, 88,
96–97

Quick Grass, 192

Quickweed, Common, 92

R

Raceme, definition and
example, 17

Ragweed, Common (Annual)
and Western, **56–57**, 143

Ragweed, Giant (Great),
58–59, 143

Ragwort, Common, 110

Ranunculus abortivus,
sceleratus, **112–113**

Ranunculus acris, hispidus,
130–131

Ray flowers, about and
examples, 14, 16

Red Clover, **32–33**

Red-Root Amaranth, 66

Red-Seeded Dandelion, **36**

Reniform leaves, definition
and example, 11

Resveratrol, 107

Reynoutria japonica,
sachalinensis, **106–107**

Rhaponticum repens, **168**

Rhizomes, definition, 8

Rhombic Copperleaf, 102

Rhomboid Mercury, 102

Rhubarb, Wild, 162

Rhus radicans, 60, 174

Ridge-Seed Spurge, **28**

Rocket, Yellow, **108–109**

Rough Avens, **74**

Rough Cinquefoil, **132–133**

Rough Pigweed, 62, **66–67**

Round-Leaved Mallow, 148

Round leaves, definition and
example, 11

Rumex altissimus, crispus,
122–123

Russian Knapweed, **168**

Rusty Woodsia, **24**

S

Sandmats, 28

Scentless False Mayweed, 44

Securigera varia, **154–155**

Seedhead, example, 15

Seedpods, example, 15

Senecio vulgaris, **110–111**

Sepals, definition and
examples, 14–15

Sessile leaf attachment,
definition and example, 13

Setaria faberi, italica, pumila,
viridis, **194–195**

Shaggy Soldier, 92

Shallowly lobed leaves,
definition and example, 11

Shepherd's Purse, **80–81**

Showy Milkweed, 158

Sicyos angulatus, lobata,
184–185

Silene csereii, latifolia,
vulgaris, **86–87**

Silkweed, 158

Silver Cinquefoil, **34–35**

Silver Crabgrass, 200

Sinapis genus, 108

Sisymbrium genus, 108

Six-Weeks Grass, 190

Skunkgrass, 204

Slender Amaranth, **66**

Small Crabgrass, 196

Small-Flowered
Buttercup, 112

Small-Flowered Galinsoga,
92–93

Smartweed, 150
Nodding (Pale) and
Pennsylvania, **150–151**

Smooth Amaranth, 66

Smooth Brome, **192**

Smooth Crabgrass, **196**, 200

Smooth Goldenrod, 142

Smooth Pigweed, 66

Snakeroot, White, **104–105**

Snapdragon, Wild, 128

Soil amendments, 21

Solanum carolinense, rostratum, **84–85**

Solanum dulcamara, **186–187**

Solanum nigrum, ptycanthum, ptychanthum, **94–95**

Solidago altissima, canadensis, gigantea, **142–143**

Sonchus arvensis, asper, oleraceus, **136–137**

Sourgrass, 120

Sowthistles (several), 36, **136–137**

Spear Grass, 190

Spear Thistle, 164

Speedwell, Corn, **54–55**

Spike, definition and example, 17

Spiked Loosestrife, 170

Spinach, Wild, 62

Spiny Amaranth, **66**

Spiny Sowthistle (Prickly Sowthistle), **136–137**

Spotted Knapweed, **168–169**

Spotted Ladysthumb, 150

Spotted Spurge, **28–29**

Spotted St. John's Wort, **124**

Spurge, Cypress and Leafy, 98, **118–119**

Spurges, Low-Growing (several), **28–29**, 30, 46

Stamen, definition and example, 14–15

Standard (petal), definition, 16

Stellaria media, **26**

Stigma, definition and examples, 14–15, 16

Stinging Nettle, **64–65**, 102

Stinkgrass, **204–205**

Stinking Chamomile, 90

Stinkweed, 68

St. John's Wort, Common (St. Johnswort), **124–125**

Stolons, definition, 9

Strawberry, Mock (Indian), **38–39**

Strawberry Weed, 132

Strawberry, wild, **38**

Straw-Colored Flatsedge, **198**

Style, definition and examples, 14–15, 16

Sulfur Cinquefoil, **132–133**

Sweet-Clover, Yellow and White, **116–117**

T

Tall Beggar's Ticks, **144–145**

Tall Boneset, 104

Tall Buttercup, **130–131**

Tall Goldenrod, 142

Tall Morning Glory, 188

Tanacetum vulgare, **140–141**

Tansy, **140–141**

Tansy, Wild (as name for Common Ragweed), 56

Taraxacum erythrospermum, officinale, vulgare, **36–37**

Tea, weeds used for, 33, 39, 45, 49, 53, 99, 125, 135, 157, 167

Teardrop-shaped leaves, definition and example, 10

Teucrium canadense, **166**

Textiles, weeds used to produce, 65

Thayer, Sam, 115

Thistle
  Bull (Spear, Black), **164–165**
  Canada (Field), **160–161**, 168
  Field, **160–161**
  Nodding, **164–165**
  Plumeless, **164–165**

Thlaspi arvense, **68–69**

Three-Seeded Mercury, **102–103**

Throw-Wort, 152

Toadflax, 98
  Dalmatian, **128**
  Yellow, **128–129**

Toxicodendron radicans, **174–175**

Toxicodendron rydbergii, **60–61**

Trailing Crownvetch, 154

Trefoil, Birdsfoot (Yellow), 16, **126–127**

Trifoliate leaves, definition and example, 12

Trifolium aureum, campestre, **42**

Trifolium hybridum, pratense, repens, **32–33**

Trionum trionum, 100

Tripleurospermum inodorum, **44**

Tubers, definition, 9

Tufted Lovegrass, **204**

Tufted seeds, example, 15

Twice-compound leaves, definition and example, 12

U

Umbel, definition and example, 17

Umbrella Wort, 156

Urtica dioica, **64–65**

Urushiol, 61

V

Velvet Plant, 134

Venice Mallow, **100–101**

Verbascum thapsus, **134–135**

Verbena, Big-Bract, **54–55**

Verbena bracteata, **54–55**

Veronica arvensis, **54–55**

Vervain, Prostrate, 54

Vetch, Crown and Common, **154–155**

Vicia sativa, **154**

Viola canadensis, pubescens, sororia, **48–49**

Violets (several), **48–49**, 70
Virginia Copperleaf, **102**
Virginia Creeper, **178–179**
Virginia Peppergrass or
  Pepperweed, 72
Vitis spp., **178**

W

Water Chickweed, **26**
Watergrass, 198
Waterpod, 24
Waterweed, 24
Western Poison Ivy, **60–61**
Western Ragweed, **56**
West Indian Nightshade, 94
White Avens, **74–75**
White Campion, **86–87**
White Clover, 16, **32–33**
White Cockle, 86
White Four o'Clock, 156
White Snakeroot, **104–105**
White Sweet-Clover, **116**
Whitetop, 68
Whorled Chickweed, 30

Whorled leaf arrangement,
  definition and example, 13
Wild Balsam Apple, 184
Wild Buckwheat, 176
Wild Carrot, 96
Wild Chamomile, 44
Wild Cucumber, **184–185**
Wild Four o'Clock, **156–157**
Wild Grapes, **178**
Wild Lettuce, 138
Wild Millet, 194
Wild Mint, **152–153**
Wild Morning Glory, 182
Wild Parsnip, 78, 79, **114–115**
Wild Rhubarb, 162
Wild Rye, Canada, **192**
Wild Snapdragon, 128
Wild Spinach, 62
Wild Strawberry, **38**
Wild Tansy, 56
Wine, weeds used to
  make, 37
Wing petals, definition, 16
Winter Cress, 108
Wiregrass, 200

Witchgrass, 192
Woodbine, **178–179**
Wood Nettle, **64**
Woodsia ilvensis, **24**
Woodsia, Rusty, **24**
Wood Sorrel, Yellow
  (Woodsorrel), **120–121**

Y

Yarrow (Common), **88–89**
Yellow Avens, **74**
Yellow Bristle Grass, 194
Yellow Dock, 122
Yellow Foxtail, **194–195**
Yellow Loosestrife,
  Creeping, 40
Yellow Melilot, 116
Yellow Nutsedge, **198–199**
Yellow Rocket, **108–109**
Yellow Sweet-Clover,
  116–117
Yellow Toadflax, **128–129**
Yellow Trefoil, 126
Yellow Violet, Downy, **48–49**
Yellow Wood Sorrel, **120–121**

A NOTE ABOUT CONSUMING WILD PLANTS

Numerous plants in this book have parts (such as leaves, stems or roots) that are consumed by many foragers, or used to make things such as jelly, tea or wine. Before consuming any part of a plant you've gathered from the wild, you must be *absolutely certain* of its identity. Study all ID characteristics in this book, and also consult a book on foraging for additional identification points; if possible, also get guidance from a knowledgeable forager. Always keep these points in mind:

• Never gather plants in an area that has been chemically treated (for example, fertilizer or weed killer). Also gather well away from roads, to avoid possible contamination from fumes and dust which may contain harmful substances.

• Remember that only certain parts of a plant may be edible, and only at the proper stage. Many wild plants must be cooked before eating. Consult a reliable resource for guidance on preparing wild plants.

• Be aware that some plants may cause an allergic reaction, or may disagree with some individuals. Sample only a small portion the first time you try a new plant.

ABOUT THE AUTHOR

Teresa Marrone is the author of more than a dozen outdoors-themed books, including the *Wild Berries & Fruits Field Guide* series (currently available for four regions of the U.S.) and a new series of mushroom ID guides; see below for more information. She has also written numerous cookbooks about wild foods, and has been gathering and preparing wild edibles for three decades. Teresa lives in Minneapolis with husband Bruce and enjoys shooting photos of mushrooms, berries, other plants and all things wild in the area surrounding their property abutting Minnesota's Boundary Waters Canoe Area Wilderness.